ACTIVE GOODNESS

THE TRUE STORY OF HOW TREVOR CHADWICK, DOREEN WARRINER & NICHOLAS WINTON SAVED THOUSANDS FROM THE NAZIS

Edward Abel Smith

First Paperback Edition 2017 Kwill Books

www.kwillbooks.com

ISBN-13: 978-84-947548-5-2

YOUNG**ROOTS**

Proceeds of this book go to Young Roots

http://youngroots.org.uk

UK Registered Charity No. 1139685 — UK Company No. 7448744

FOR GEORGINA

There is a difference between passive goodness and active goodness. The latter is, in my opinion, the giving of one's time and energy in the alleviation of pain and suffering. It entails going out, finding and helping those who are suffering and in danger and not merely in leading an exemplary life, in a purely passive way of doing no wrong.

Sir Nicholas Winton[1]

TABLE OF CONTENTS

IN HONOUR OF

WITHOUT WHOM,
THOUSANDS WOULD NOT
HAVE SURVIVED

Doreen Warriner
Wenzel Jaksch
Siegfried Taub
John Ingman

Walter Layton
Mary Penman
Arthur Salter
Christine Maxwell

Robin Hankey
Ronald Kidd
Barbara Willis

Nicholas Winton
David Grenfell
Harold Gibson
Hilde Patz

David Willis
Ewart Cuplin
Victor Cazalet
Margaret Dougan

Bill Barazetti
Geoff Phelps
Alois Mollik

Trevor Chadwick
William Gillies
Tessa Rowntree
Margaret Layton

Martin Blake
Alec Dickson
Eleanor Rathbone
Robert Stopford

Harold Hales
Barbara Winton
Douglas Reed

CHAPTER 1

INTRODUCTION

Ten-year-old Vera Gissing was on a train. It was one hour into its journey and the clock had just ticked past midnight. The carriage was dark and crowded with children between the ages of three and fifteen. Strangely there were no adults, and not even her parents. As the dark countryside raced by, the train was screeching its way out of these children's home country, Czechoslovakia.

Vera and her companions were on one of eight such trains, hurtling from Prague, through Poland, to London Liverpool Street. In total, 669 children made this journey over the space of four months in 1939.

All these children came from different backgrounds and had little in common, but what they did share was not being aware of exactly where they were going and more importantly, why. What they also did not know was that they would most likely never see their parents again. Nor would they ever see any of the 15,000 other children from their country who were not chosen to be on one of these trains.

The reason – they were all murdered over the next six years for having one thing in common: Being Jewish.

63 years later, now aged 73, Vera addressed a large audience in Westminster Central Hall, London on 27th January 2001. Every year around the world on this day is the Inaugural National Commemoration, known as the Holocaust Memorial Day. She recalled her first meeting with her new foster-mother at London Liverpool Street station when she arrived off the train in 1939: "Her first words (to Vera) were 'you shall be loved.' And those are the most important words any refugee child needs to hear."[2]

Vera was at Westminster Central Hall to introduce a man called Sir Nicholas Winton as the special guest for the event. He was the man who had helped organise for her to be on that train. "As one of the child refugees from Prague," she said, "I owe my life to Nicholas, but he could not have succeeded without the help of others."[3]

A lot has been reported and written about Sir Nicholas Winton and if you were to believe the common myth, he worked alone to organise the escape of Vera and her companions. This is so far from the truth that Winton himself spent much of his latter life trying to dismiss this illusion. "Most of the credit should go to others," he said in one of his many speeches, adding, "in a way I shouldn't have lived so long to give everyone the opportunity to exaggerate in the way they are doing today."[4]

The others he referred to sat on all possible peripheries of society including a teacher, a diplomat, a travel agent, a spy, a passport officer, a British Cabinet Minister, the son of a Vicar, a man on the run and a PhD lecturer. Each of these individuals deserve equal recognition and praise for the bravery, dedication and sacrifices they made to save Vera and so many others.

However, when researching the remarkable story of Sir Nicholas, there were two names which jumped out time and time again over the course of the various rescue operations he was affiliated with. These were Dr Doreen Warriner and Trevor Chadwick. The former took overall leadership of all rescue operations from within Czechoslovakia, whether it was Jewish children or Socialist adults. Chadwick, a teacher, was Winton's counterpart in Prague, running the evacuation of children locally while Winton dealt with British end.

The three – Nicholas Winton, Doreen Warriner and Trevor Chadwick – shared many traits. They were all adroit, adventurous, brave, incredibly determined, and ultimately they were great humanitarians. But they were also widely different in personality. Chadwick was somewhat a lady's man, wonderfully eccentric and shied away from authority. Warriner was painfully honest, stubborn and often irresponsibly impulsive. Winton was calm, a deep thinker, and usually reserved. Despite their differences they worked effectively together and were the perfect complement to each other. All three were also astonishingly modest about what they achieved which accounts in part for why their story has remained in the peripheries of the history books.

To truly understand the efforts of these three exceptional individuals and their many collaborators, we need to canter through the immediate history of Czechoslovakia at the time. Then we must explore why so many people were in imminent danger of persecution and death. Only after truly contextualising this can we understand the events which these three orchestrated.

In simple terms, Warriner concentrated on the escape of political refugees and Winton focused on the rescue of Jewish children, with Chadwick provided support to them both. Warriner has been criticised for only helping those who were being persecuted for their political beliefs rather than their religious beliefs. She has also been criticised for not rescuing children, with Chadwick's son later noting that "what Winton saw almost immediately was that the children had to be his priority because they were nobody else's."[5]

The truth is that Warriner did originally focus on the men in danger, then their wives and children as a second priority. But if this is contextualised to the time, the main threat the Nazis posed in 1938 was against those who opposed Hitler's policy and the ethics of the Third Reich. Many of the infamous concentration camps to emerge from WWII, such as Auschwitz, were built for this clientele. Clearly the European Jews were, to say the very least, in an uncomfortable situation, but in 1938, they were being encouraged to leave Europe. It was only in early 1942 that the Nazis' infamous "Final Solution" was inaugurated. So, although there was no doubt that the Jewish community was in immense danger, the full scale of their destruction was less apparent than of those who openly spoke out in opposition of Hitler and his ideals.

Winton has received a fair amount of recognition for his part in the rescue and has rightly become a household name because of it, but Warriner and Chadwick have not. It is likely that the reason for Winton receiving more recognition was because he lived to the astonishing age of 106, outliving the other two by some margin.

It is with hope that this book sheds light on the contribution of all three in equal measure. There is no deliberate attempt to dilute the work of Nicholas Winton by raising the profiles of Warriner and Chadwick. All the credit which has gone Winton's way is fully and completely deserved.

CHAPTER 2

BETRAYED BY THEIR ALLIES

"An appeaser is one who feeds a crocodile hoping
it will eat him last."
Sir Winston Churchill[6]

As the 1930s ensued, it was becoming evident to many that a wide-ranging European war was on its way for the second time that century. This growing feeling was born out of the post-World War I oppression in Germany and the emergence of the National Socialist German Workers' Party, the Nazi party, led by Adolf Hitler.

With his mind set on world domination, Hitler's first act of international aggression was to annexe Austria on 12th March 1938. This was a direct contravention to the Treaty of Versailles, the peace agreement signed after World War I in 1919, which specifically prohibited the expansion of Germany and in particular, any union with Austria.

With the 38 million causalities from The Great War at the forefront of their minds, neighbouring powers were reluctant to offer any meaningful criticism to Austria's occupation. In fact, there was little protest whatsoever from the European stage. Appeasement was their only consideration.

Even when the then Chancellor of Austria, Kurt Schuschnigg, pleaded with the British and French governments to stand up for his country, there was no action from either side. The British and French leaders saw this as an international affair for which they had no responsibility, as neither had an official alliance with Austria.

Britain and France did have a treaty with other countries surrounding Germany, including Poland, which a year later, would be the country to force Europe back into war.

Another neighbour of Germany which Britain and France were committed to protect was Czechoslovakia.

Long part of the Austro Hungarian Empire, Czechoslovakia was founded by Tomáš Garrigue Masaryk after World War I in 1918 when the Bohemian Kingdom officially ceased to exist. The new country was a multi-ethnic state, with half the population consisting of Czechs, nearly a quarter German with the remainder including Slovaks, Hungarians, and Rusyns.

Initially after its creation in 1918, Czechoslovakia was the only newly created state to maintain its democracy, meaning it developed at a faster rate than those other states created from a post war broken Europe. It was for this reason, among others, that Hitler had his sights on the country as his next conquest.

Part of the newly formed Czechoslovakia was the Sudetenland, which bordered with Germany. This area had been confiscated from Germany after they surrendered in 1918 and was therefore predominantly populated by native Germans, many of whom were angry at being separated from their home country.

Hitler believed the Sudetenland had been stolen. While addressing his party conference in 1938, he demanded that "the oppression of three and a half million Germans in Czechoslovakia cease and that the inalienable right to self-determination take its place."[7]

Within the Sudetenland, feelings were divided. The two opposing groups were the pro-Nazi Sudeten German Party (SdP) and the anti-Nazi German Social Democratic Workers Party in the Czechoslovak Republic, simply known as the Sudeten Social Democrats. Both parties had considerable support and violently opposed each other.

Two weeks after assuming control of Austria, Konrad Henlein, the leader of the SdP travelled to Berlin for a pre-arranged appointment with Hitler. On 28th March 1938 they met to discuss how the SdP would be able to help the Nazis take control of the Sudetenland and incorporate it into The Third Reich.

Henlein returned to Czechoslovakia with a monthly allowance of 15,000 marks from Germany to fund the activities of the SdP. In return, Joachim von Ribbentrop, the newly appointed Reich Minister for Foreign Affairs in Germany, brought the SdP under his direct control. Henlein was instructed by Hitler and Ribbentrop to demand the autonomy of the Sudetenland from the Czechoslovak government, led by president Edvard Beneš.

Beneš did not take the ultimatum presented before him too seriously, for his country had powerful allies who were committed to securing their safety. He was wrong to put so much faith and trust in these allies, as they were about to betray him.

Setting his party members to work, Henlein led a campaign of unrest throughout the Sudetenland, setting unachievable demands on Beneš known as the Carlsbad Program. The Czech government were only able to offer some token gestures to the SdP, which did little to suppress the uprising. Hitler made it clear that these demands not being met was an act of aggression against his people and Germany. He therefore began to draw up plans to invade the Sudetenland.

Desperate to avoid any bloodshed, British Prime Minster Neville Chamberlain flew to Berlin to discuss the situation with Hitler. Negotiations continued for several weeks, culminating in a meeting of several European leaders at the Munich Conference 29th September 1938. Conversations continued into the early hours of the following day until an agreement was reached. Hitler had got what he wanted – the European leaders agreed to allow a break in the terms of the Treaty of Versailles and to give Germany control of the Sudetenland. Not invited to the conference, Beneš was not consulted on this decision.

In return, the European leaders present sought assurance that this deal would ensure no further conflict. Neville Chamberlain, famously asked Hitler at this agreement to sign a peace treaty between Germany and the United Kingdom. This signature was worth less than the paper it was written on and the Sudetenland was used as a bargaining chip and sacrificed for no meaningful reason.

Nevertheless, Chamberlain returned to Heston Aerodrome in Britain where he delivered his infamous "peace for our time" speech, stating that, "the Anglo-German Naval Agreement is symbolic of the desire of our two peoples never to go to war with one another again. This is the second time in our history that there has come back from Germany to Downing Street peace with honour."[8] As history shows, this was far from the truth. It was not as Chamberlain referred to the affair as "a quarrel in a faraway country between people we know nothing about..."[9]

Reaction from the world stage was mixed. Looking back on the appeasement, Winston Churchill stated, "It is a mystery and tragedy of European history that a people capable of every heroic virtue, gifted, valiant, charming, as individuals, should repeatedly show such inveterate faults in almost every aspect of their governmental life."[10]

Even Russian dictator Joseph Stalin was perplexed by the outcomes of the Munich Conference, concluding that the West had actively colluded with Hitler, which in some ways, they had.

For Hitler and the Third Reich, the Sudetenland was the start of their conquest of Czechoslovakia for, not only was it further territory for Germany but it also had strategic value. Rich in industry, the country would go on to be used by the Nazis to produce weapons and ammunition. In years to come, by occupying the whole of Czechoslovakia, Germany was able to construct an extra 2,175 field cannons, 469 tanks, 500 anti-aircraft artillery pieces, 43,000 machine guns, 1,090,000 military rifles, 114,000 pistols, three million anti-aircraft grenades and approximately a billion rounds of ammunition. History shows that the Munich Agreement would go on to have devastating consequences for the British during the War, heavily arming their enemy.

On 30th September, the Sudetenland was swallowed up by the Third Reich. The Nazi-led SdP party was now in power. They focused their hatred on those who had opposed them over the years, terrorising members and supporters of the Sudeten Social Democrat party in particular.

Fearing for their safety, thousands of men, women, and children fled across the border to seek refuge in what was left of Czechoslovakia from the inevitable Nazi terror. It is estimated that between 150,000 and 200,000 people left their homes and headed to Prague, which presented a dilemma for the residents of Prague and the surrounding area. Of the nearly 200,000 recently displaced individuals, over 90% were Czech by background and were shown more sympathy by the locals. A lot of the Czech refugees were offered spare rooms, farm buildings or any other form of shelter, where they were able to live in relative comfort.

Residents for several reasons were unable to offer the same hospitality the remaining 10%, who were mostly German. This was partly because they were seen to represent the enemy to the Czech people and were therefore not trusted. A more obvious reason, suggested by leading British politicians at the time, was the "unwillingness of its Government to retain within its shrunken borders men of German race (with) anti-Nazi opinions who are likely to be the cause of friction with the German Government."[11] Because of this, the general mentality by the Czechs was that German refugees should be settled in a different country altogether and were therefore in Prague as a temporary measure. Logistically as well, there was simply a lack of space to house everyone permanently, meaning around 20,000 people were having to make do with refugee camps which were being erected around Prague - usually old schools, castles or village halls.

The three largest camps were Světlá Castle, Dolná Krupá Castle and Nížkov village school. Housing the most people, these three camps were incredibly overcrowded and quickly conditions became borderline inhabitable, without heating or much food. As winter encroached, the refugees who now called these camps home had to struggle on without basic amenities of coal, straw or blankets to keep warm.

CHAPTER 3

THE PERSECUTED

"The stronger must dominate and not mate with the weaker,
which would signify the sacrifice of its own
higher nature. Only the born weakling can look upon this
principle as cruel, and if he does so it is merely
because he is of a feebler nature and narrower mind."
Adolf Hitler[12]

Jews, disabled people, communists, homosexuals, degenerate artists, prostitutes, black people, intellectuals, philosophers, alcoholics, teachers, social democrats, Jehovah's Witnesses, gypsies, asocials, Roman Catholics, Freemasons, overweight people, vagrants, drug addicts, open dissidents, pacifists, Non-Europeans... These are just some of the many areas of society Hitler detested.

They were, he believed, not welcome in his Aryan territory and therefore needed removing, by whatever means possible. Through his many speeches over the years, and his book, *Mein Kampf* (*My Struggle*), published in two volumes between 1925 and 1926, his prejudices were well known.

Not one to be picky, Hitler would discriminate against all. Within Czechoslovakia, there were two groups who he would go on to target the most.

The first were the Jews, well known to be Hitler's favourite hate group, resulting in one of the most horrific acts of human cruelty in recent history.

The Holocaust – the genocidal killing of over six million Jews, nearly a third of whom were children – took place across the continent between 1941 and Germany's defeat in May 1945. With nine million Jews living in Europe at the time; two thirds of the religion's population were wiped off the face of the continent. Hitler made no secret of his cruel intentions to persecute this group.

In the build-up to this hideous time in history, things went from bad to worse for German Jews, who were being increasingly targeted since Hitler took the reins of Germany in 1933. He stated his mission was to "alert Germany and the world" to the threat against Aryan culture by "Hebrew corrupters of the people."[13]

What started as sporadic attacks by Nazi supporters, led to regular beatings of Jews by Hitler's Stormtroopers. Incited hatred continued, culminating with the establishment of Dachau concentration camp in March 1933. This vast construction was the first of its kind, and could accommodate up to 25,000 inmates. Nearly all housed there would be Jewish.

For the next five years, the discrimination and violence against German Jews was gradual, but drastic and brutal. For those in Europe with a Jewish heritage, at the very least life was uncomfortable, and for some incredibly dangerous. However, the sound of jackboots goose-stepping into Austria on 13th March 1938 signalled a new era of devastation for the religion. The persecution of the Austrian Jews was instant and had hideous consequences. By the following day, 14th March, all Jews in Austria were stripped of their civil rights and were immediately subjected to extreme levels of violence and humiliation.

By July 1938, the rise of anti-Semitic violence and the subsequent fleeing of Jews, meant foreign powers could not ignore the situation any longer, leading to an emergency international conference in Evian, Switzerland.

With government representatives from 31 countries present, Jewish civilians around the continent held their breath for a solution to this religious discrimination. Optimism was particularly high as there were so many democratic countries in attendance.

So what was the outcome of this international crisis conference? In a word; nothing. So fearful were European powers of further bloodshed that the governments present showed a complete reluctance to partake in any military action whatsoever. With this off the table, conversations turned to offering a place of refuge for the persecuted. In response to this idea, each government present in Evian, one by one, began using their own domestic problems as an excuse why they could not increase their refugee quota.

For Britain, low employment levels and the post Great War depression were quoted as the reasons for their borders remaining restricted. An anonymous person present at the conference remarked at the close of proceedings how the word 'Evian' was simply 'naïve' spelled backwards. Until further notice, the persecuted Jews were on their own.

The 1930 census showed that over 350,000 people in Czechoslovakia identified themselves as Jewish by religion, spread between the provinces of Bohemia, Moravia, and Slovakia, many of whom were German Jews living in The Sudetenland. Terrified for their safety, the Sudeten Jews fled from their homes across the new border into Czechoslovakia and headed for the capital in the hope of safety.

The second Sudeten group in notable danger were those who opposed or spoke publicly against the Nazi regime and ideals. Loathed by Hitler and his inner circles, they classed these individuals as a threat to the future of Fascism.

A further five million non-Jewish people were victims of targeted killings during the Nazi reign, and when included in the Holocaust numbers, it takes the tally of those murdered to a staggering 11 million, equivalent to the entire population of Canada at the time.

Typically very well educated, including intellectuals, doctors, lawyers, and teachers, Hitler was paranoid about these people. His prejudices were not limited to just these individuals, as he would also target those closest to them; their wives, children, parents, business associates, friends and so on.

Within The Sudetenland, many people were tarnished with this discriminatory brush. The individuals in the most immediate danger were at the forefront of anti-Nazi protest prior to the Munich Agreement – the followers of the Sudeten Social Democratic Party. It is estimated that the party had over 2,000 men who were members, many of who had large families also under threat. Similar to their Jewish neighbours, these families packed their bags and headed for the apparent safety of Prague.

Author and refugee Arthur Koestler wrote that these two groups, who he described as "people doomed by biological accident of their race (or their) rational conviction regarding the best way to organise human welfare" were now accustomed to being outcasts. [14] The government in Czechoslovakia were genuinely trying to help all they could; however the number of refugees pouring into Prague was unsustainable. The mayor, Peter Zenkl had set up camps outside the city with the Red Cross in an attempt to house them. Nevertheless, the numbers were becoming too much for the authorities to handle, leading to distressing scenes of refugees from the Sudetenland being sent back by trains, coerced on by the sharp point of a bayonet or the fierce barrel of a gun. As discussed in the previous chapter, the Czech authorities were concerned that housing German-speaking anti-Nazi people could "serve as an excuse for further intervention and territorial demands from Berlin."[15]

Because of this, these two society groups of the fallen Sudetenland who arrived in the capital city, mostly drew the short straw and were only able to receive hospitality from the state-built refugee camps. After only a couple of months, pictures and videos of the appalling deteriorating conditions these families were now living began to appear in the newspapers and news reels in Britain.

Pressure was placed on the Chamberlain administration to try and assist the refugee crisis, which critics of the government accused them of causing, a criticism which remains associated with Chamberlain to this day. Feeling the pressure to take action, on 3rd October 1938 the British government allocated £4 million to aid those in danger from the Nazi Sudetenland takeover, with a further £10 million being loaned to the Czech government. In the announcement, Chamberlain said that, "The Chancellor of the Exchequer, on the Government, has addressed a letter to the Bank of England requesting the Bank provide the necessary credit... and when the House resumes its sittings in November, Parliament will be asked to pass the necessary legislation."[16] Of this money £500,000 would be set aside to support the emigration of those deemed to be in danger.

Lynn Smith, lecturer in Human Rights and International Relations at Webster University and accomplished author on the topic believed that this was simply a way of "assuaging British guilt after the way the Czechs had been sacrificed by the British and French."[17]

Despite's Smith's belief, in November 1938, the government in Britain went even further by easing their immigration policy, following, in part, pressure from the Council for German Jewry and having witnessed the atrocities of Kristallnacht, also known as the 'night of broken glass.' This was the well planned and executed attack against Jews on the night of 9th November in Germany. Over 1,000 synagogues were burnt to the ground and 7,000 Jewish businesses attacked and looted. The relaxing of Britain's immigration policy was certainly a generous gesture in contrast to the country's previous stance four months prior at the Evian Conference.

Although the parameters were vague, it was particularly advantageous for endangered children. The rules roughly stated that children under the age of 17 were able to enter Britain from Germany and Austria, if they were deemed to be unsafe. What was not specified was the number of those who would be allowed in or what deemed a child to be "unsafe." The only condition on the numbers was that they would not be a drain on the public wallet.

The outcome of this was the creation of Operation Kindertransport, or now known simply as Kindertransport.

This was a merger of a section of Central British Fund for World Jewish Relief, called the Refugee Children's Movement and various other Jewish, Quaker and Christian charities and groups.

With the anticipation that the suffering would soon escalate, the operation needed major funding. This came from the generosity of the British people, organised by a man called Stanley Baldwin, named the Earl Baldwin Fund. He appealed on the radio to request funding as follows, "I ask you to come to the aid of victims not of any catastrophe in the natural world, not of earthquake, not of flood, not of famine, but of an explosion of Man's inhumanity to Man."[18] The Earl Baldwin Fund was filled by generous donations and rose to over £500,000. Of this, just under a half, £200,000 was allocated to Kindertransport. Between 3rd December 1938 and 3rd September 1939, the day war was declared on the Nazis by the Allies, nearly 10,000 endangered children had been removed from Austria and Germany and taken to the safety of Britain. Of these, over 1,000 men and women would go on to be old enough to enlist into the British Forces and return to the occupied territories they had fled. Of these, 30 lost their lives fighting the Nazis.

Despite the £500,000 funding, the relaxing of border controls and the creation of Kindertransport, the Czech refugees felt little impact in late 1938 or early 1939. The donation was not finalised and released until February 1939, over four months after the refugee camps in Prague began to fill up. As for the relaxed border controls, each immigrant needed over £50 to enter Britain, meaning that only the wealthy were able to take advantage of this, until the British donation was handed over. Finally, for some reason there were groups getting hundreds of children out of Germany and Austria, but no support or interest in Czechoslovakia. The sad truth is that Czechoslovakia was not included within the remit of the Kindertransport. As Vera Gissing asked: "What about the threatened children from Czechoslovakia?" [19] Likely because events in the country escalated so rapidly and the charities were already stretched.

Of the 356,830 Jews in Czechoslovakia, the Nazis and their collaborators would go on to kill nearly 263,000. The majority were sent to Theresienstadt concentration camp, before being transported to their deaths at Treblinka and Auschwitz extermination camps in occupied Poland. Any Sudeten Democrats arrested were also sent through Theresienstadt to their death. Among those who died of poor conditions or were executed there was Esther Adolphine, sister of Sigmund Freud, dying on 29th September 1942.

From the takeover of the Sudetenland in early October 1938 and the declaration of war on Germany on 3rd September 1939, the fate of the endangered in Czechoslovakia was not in the hands of any country's governments. It fell to the mercy of certain individuals. Three of whom would go on to lead rescue operations – all of them had had to take the situation into their own hands.

CHAPTER 4

TREVOR CHADWICK

"My daughter once said to me, 'so you realise Mummy that
if it were not for Trevor Chadwick, I wouldn't exist.'"
Margit Fazakerley[20]

Trevor Chadwick was born on 22nd April 1907 into a family of four siblings. As the second youngest in the family, he knew little of his father, who died just five years after he was born. His father had founded Forres Prep School, in Swanage which he ran up until his death in 1912 and was succeeded by his brother, Rev. R.M. Chadwick.

Trevor's son, William, who wrote an excellent book on the topic recalled how "it was openly agreed by all members of the family that he became his mother's favourite and was horribly spoilt."[21] He attended the Dragon School, a private school in Oxford, founded in 1877 by a group of Oxford Dons. As one of the top schools of its type in Britain, it is known for its unconventional approach to education, based on the idea of children having an awareness and understanding of the world around them.

As Old Dragon and former civil servant Peter Bourne wrote: "The absence of rigid regimentation at the Dragon, being treated as mature beyond my years and being trusted early with significant tasks taught me self-sufficiency and the need to take responsibility for my own future from a young age. It also imbued me with tolerance and a liberal, open view of the world. I learned to appreciate the historic context into which my generation was born giving me the strong self-confidence to believe I had been prepared to achieve anything I wished in life." The attributes he describes align themselves to Chadwick and the environment was perfect for him.[22]

After a successful five years at the Dragon, it was off to senior school in Cumbria, North England. Chadwick was awarded a scholarship to Sedbergh School, a Church of England establishment, set on the boundary between the Yorkshire Dales and Lake District National Parks. This was quite a move for Chadwick, having been based near his family home in Oxford to suddenly being thrown into unfamiliar territory in another part of the country at the age of 13.

Nevertheless, his time at the school was enjoyable and fruitful, as he left with a place at Oxford University, where he spent his time captaining the college rugby team, betting on the horses and running up large bar bills – all of which were covered by his mother when needed. It would be fair to say that his track record of getting a scholarship and then a place at Oxford was not replicated during his time at the university. He graduated with a disappointing third class degree in Jurisprudence, the science, study, and theory of law.

Described by a perceptive family acquaintance as "the black sheep of a conservative Christian family,"[23] he left Oxford in 1928, and after contemplating following the family tradition of teaching at Forres, he decided on something a little less conventional. With a flair for adventure, he joined the Colonial Services as a district officer and with his first assignment he was sent to Nigeria. The Colonial Services was a government led initiative, whose function was to manage the country's colonies, as part of the Secretary of State for the Colonies and the Colonial Office in Westminster. According the colony's annual report in 1930 (around a year after he joined), Nigeria was larger than any other British dependency, excluding Tanganyika and India, at approximately 373,078 square miles (over three times the size of the United Kingdom) and a population of over 18 million. Although there were some incidents of violence, most notably the death of Assistant District Officer Barlow on 8th February 1930 caused by an attack from locals, the colony was stable with production and exports thriving.[24]

The role of a district officer at that time was to act as the bridge between the colonial government and the people within the district. It was effectively to act as the local spokesman for both sides of the operation. As a commissioned officer, this role would have promised Chadwick a fruitful career if he played his cards right, with the prospect of becoming a colonial governor; the highest rank in the Colonial Services of whom there were only 40 at the time.

However his time as a district officer was a short one, leaving after just 18 months in Nigeria. It is likely that he resigned because he had fallen in love with a woman. Prior to his departure to Nigeria, he had spent much of his time with his younger brother, Huge, who was farming near Battle, a small parish town in East Sussex, England and once the venue for William, Duke of Normandy's defeat over King Harold II in 1066 at the Battle of Hastings. The farmer from whom Huge was employed, had a "beautiful daughter" who became somewhat of a fascination for Trevor.[25] It is believed that she would have been the reason for his return visits to the farm before he left for Nigeria.

In 1931, they were married. Life as the wife of the district officer in Nigeria, which as we have seen, had its dangers, would not have been as glamorous as it might sound. As the role would have involved lots of regional travel, it would mean the wives would often be left for weeks on their own, in a part of the world where they would not have friends to keep them company. This was obviously before the time of rapid communication, which meant that the yearning for home was great and young wives would struggle being cut off from their families. This was a concern to Trevor, and it seems that it was with little thought that he resigned his role in Nigeria so as not to subject his wife to that lifestyle.

Upon his return, he fell back on the family business and no doubt to the delight of the Chadwicks, he joined Forres as a Latin teacher. At this point of his story, it may seem that Chadwick would settle down with his new wife in his new job as part of the family business. This was not the case. It was hoped by his uncle that he could take over the reins as headmaster, following in his father's footsteps, however it soon became apparent that he was not suitable to the task.

There were certain traits which were tolerated and even celebrated by certain people. For example arriving to the parents' evening in fancy dress as an ice cream salesman, selling the frozen treats to the children and their parents. Another time, he arrived to Latin class with a completely shaved head and with no explanation or any sign of embarrassment, he taught the lesson. However, there were stories which were less harmless and could not just be put down to eccentricity. Chadwick had become close friends with the coxswain of the local lifeboat crew, Bob Brown who also happened to be the landlord at the nearby Black Swan pub. Unfortunately, alcohol became a factor in Chadwick's life, leading him to turn up late to class, straight from the pub or from the fishing with his friends, and on several occasions, he would not turn up at all.

With all his shortfalls, Chadwick certainly made up for them with generosity and kindness. He volunteered for the Swanage lifeboat crew, arranged for buses for locals to be able to attend sporting events and even arranged parties for less advantaged children. His generosity of character to those around him did however come at a cost and this was to his wife. With so much time spent at the bar of the Black Swan, fishing with friends and supporting the local community, it left little time for him to be at home with his wife or include her in his social calendar. For her, this was a miserable time, during which she felt alone. The very lifestyle which Chadwick had tried to avoid for her in Nigeria, was sadly becoming a reality for her in Britain. William Chadwick quotes her as saying: "His life was pubbing... his close friends were the local fishermen – he preferred that type and they hero-worshiped him."[26]

Nevertheless, they remained married for the eight years he was teaching at Forres, without any recorded incident of them separating at any point. It was towards the end of 1938, when news was starting to filter through the papers and radio of the persecution of Jews, and many others, following the rise of the Nazi party. There were many stories of children escaping from Germany and Austria and coming to Britain for their safety.

It was at this time that appeals for sponsorship began to appear and in particular the church networks were busy in this regard. It is likely that Trevor's uncle and headmaster of

Forres, Rev R.M. Chadwick would have received such an appeal through his church. In any case, he decided that the school would be able to take two children. It is not certain why he chose that these children should come from Czechoslovakia rather than Austria or Germany, but in any case, that was his chosen location. He needed someone to go out there to help choose and escort these children back and who better suited than his adventurous and maverick nephew, Trevor.

CHAPTER 5

NICHOLAS WINTON

"It's wonderful that (Winton) was able
to save so many children."
HRH Queen Elizabeth II[27]

Born Nicholas (Nicky) George Wertheim on 19th May 1909, Nicky was the middle child of three to parents Rudolf and Babette. His elder sister, Lottie born Charlotte, was 20 years Nicholas' senior and the youngest, Robert, known to all as Bobby was born six years after him.

As a young German Jewish family, life was tough for the Wertheim family in the early 20th century. German heritage, however distant, would be greeted with considerable distain and suspicion. Winton's paternal grandparents, Nicholaus and Charlotte Wertheim were German-Jewish immigrants to Britain in the 1850s, moving from a town near Nürnberg, one and a half hours north of Munich.

Such was the inconvenience of the German heritage, Winton's parents Rudolf and Babette (nicknamed Babi) they changed their name from Wertheim to Winton, to make life more amenable.

Although they were a Jewish family, there is little evidence that Nicky or his family actively practiced the religion. Winton's daughter commented that "they did not attend synagogue or use any obvious Jewish religious rituals at home."[28] In fact, all three children were baptised into the Church of England in 1916 and Winton was later confirmed in 1925 while at school.

The Winton family lived in relative luxury in a large house which today has been converted into nine flats. Along with the family of five lived four members of staff, a cook, two maids and a nanny.

In 1916, two years into the Great War, at the age of seven, Winton attended his first school, University College School in Frognal, Hampstead. Although it was within minutes of his home, Winton was somewhat of an outsider at School. Given his German heritage, his friendship group was limited to those who were in the same boat as himself. One such friend was Stanley Murdoch who lived opposite Winton and became his closest friend.

After seven years, in 1923, Winton moved to Stowe School, Buckinghamshire. Murdoch had been the one to persuade Winton to move away from home, for what was going to be the first time in his life.

A newly formed all boy's school, the pupils lived in the magnificent Grade I listed country house, the former home of the Temple-Grenville family. The family were forced to sell the estate in 1921 due to financial difficulties, which included the 400-acre landscape garden designed by Capability Brown.

When mentioned on Stowe School's website under notable alumni, Winton is said to have been "one of the School's very first pupils when it opened in 1923" with under 100 boys in total.[29] Being neither good at sport nor academia, it would be understandable if Winton's time at School was less than remarkable. In fact, he had a whole host of unusual activities, which kept him busy. Pigeon collecting, horse riding, and fencing were three of his favourite. While he would dip his toe into the more conventional Public School activities of rugby and watching cricket, the less usual of his hobbies were his true passion.

Although there was little future with horses or pigeons, fencing was something Winton become particularly competent in. He was an integral member of the 11-man Stowe School Fencing Team, who recorded an unbeaten season in 1926, winning all five of their matches against Oxford University, University College London, and Eton, Harrow, and Westminster schools.

Academically, Winton was far from unbeaten in most of his subjects. With the exception of Maths, which he was rather good at, his results were often below par. He was, however, a determined young man and would conscientiously try to improve in the classroom.

For the headmaster and founder of the school, Mr Roxburgh, this was enough to satisfy. In Roxburgh's mind, a good pupil would leave the school being "acceptable at a dance and invaluable in a shipwreck."[30] Such a phrase could perfectly sum up Winton's ability for future life.

Although life at Stowe was comfortable for Winton, the thought of school holidays would often be the highlight of his year, showing how close he was to his parents and two siblings.

Aged 17, he finished school in 1926. He had joined as a boy and was leaving as a man. His daughter, Barbara, wrote in her excellent biography of Winton that on leaving Stowe he had developed "independence, determination and following his own instincts, based on the moral ethos of social responsibility."[31]

Financial Services was his industry of choice for his future career. This decision was inspired by his father, who had started his own career in banking, becoming a manager in 1911. Working for a bank called Japhet's, Winton joined as a clerk in early 1927. For two years, he enjoyed a routine of working eight hours a day in the bank, meeting his father for lunch and socialising with his mostly male friendship group in the evening.

After two years of the city life, Winton was posted to Germany by the bank in 1929, with both his parents taking him over to settle him in.

Soon, he was back on the road and headed for Paris on another posting. These two European stays had the advantage of not only giving Winton a wider perspective on the political volatilely in the continent, but also giving him valuable language skills in both German and French.

With a shortage of employees with such international experience, Winton was immediately employed upon his return to Britain by another bank, Anglo-Czech but he was soon snapped up again in 1937 by the prestigious Stock Exchange. As a stockbroker in Crews & Co, Winton was in a much more exciting environment trading international gold stocks.

After a year in this job, instead of going on a well-deserved skiing holiday, Winton got a call to travel to Prague on a three-week voyage that people still talk about 80 years later.

CHAPTER 6

DOREEN WARRINER

"The efforts made…the decency…the courage…the humanity
demonstrated by Warriner are rarefied.
Such devotion is seldom witnessed."
Gary Levine [32]

Doreen Agnes Rosemary Julia Warriner was born into a middle-class farming family in Warwickshire on March 16th 1904. Her father had begun his career as a land agent, before progressing into estate management roles. He then became a landlord in his own right. Her mother remained at home as the children grew up.

Neither of her parents demonstrated the flare for social conscience in the same way Warriner went on to show. Perhaps the foundation of her passion could well have come from past generations in her mother's family. Indeed, her maternal grandfather was a priest from a poor parish in Staffordshire, Ireland. He had been a prominent voice in the Fenian Brotherhood and the Irish Republican Brotherhood, both of which were founded in 1858 as a rebellion to the Great Famine in Ireland in the 1840s, which had caused the death of one million nationals and the displacement of a further million. Having staged multiple revolts and attempted coups, the IRB eventually dissolved itself in 1924, with members being incorporated into what became the IRA. Back in its earlier days, Warriner's grandfather was an active member of the IRB, which led to him fleeing Ireland to avoid arrest and settling in Warwickshire.

In her early teenage years Warriner was already running the family farm, having taken control from her father who was not fit enough to continue. Her ability to step up to a challenge, no matter the scale or her own situation at the time, was something she continued to do through her life. Her time running the farm also taught her from an early age how to manage her time and quickly solve problems.

She attended Malvern Girls' College, situated in Great Malvern, Worcestershire. During her time there, the school was growing, in particular with the purchase of the local Imperial Hotel after WWI, nearly doubling in size. Some of the girls found this dramatic change in culture difficult, but Warriner simply took it in her stride.

The school clearly had a strong impact on its students, encouraging the girls not to follow the assumed path for females at the time, describing itself as "an inspirational climate which encourages risk-taking and sets high expectations."[33]

One of Warriner's peers at the school was Elizabeth Lane, who went on to become the first female High Court Judge in England, assigned to the Probate, Divorce and Admiralty

Division and awarded the female equivalent of a knighthood. It is perhaps this type of person who inspired Warriner to take a somewhat unconventional route as a woman in those times and go on to study at university. Although they did not meet, soon after Warriner left Malvern Girls' College, it was attended by future politician Peggy Jay who was a force to be reckoned with in Parliament.

Upon leaving the school, Warriner knew the direction she wanted her life to go in. She was not interested in following in the footsteps of her mother by remaining at home to look after a family, nor did she did want to follow her father's footsteps either. She wanted to move into academia as a career – one which very few women had done before her.

Warriner managed to secure herself a place at St Hugh's College, Oxford to read Philosophy, Politics, and Economics. True to her form, the college was founded in 1886 by Elizabeth Wordsworth, the great-niece of poet William Wordsworth, designed for less affluent female undergraduates. Several decades after Warriner's time at the college it was attended by a young politically-minded woman, Theresa May, who went on to become Prime Minister of the United Kingdom at the time of writing this book.

In her St Hugh's Day 1928 speech, College Principal Barbara Gwyer announced the "pleasant success" of Warriner's election in the Mary Somerville Research Fellowship at Summerville College.[34] Gwyer was an impressive woman who ran the college from October 1924 to October 1945, seeing the place change dramatically in that time. Her calming demeanour was influential on all the women who passed through the college under her tenure. She oversaw the requisition of the college buildings by the War Office following the outbreak of WWII. Once a steady and peaceful atmosphere for studying, the buildings became the hub for brain injuries and neurological research for the duration, led by celebrated brain surgeon Hugh Cairns, who used the buildings for research, enabling him to drop the mortality rate of brain-penetrating injuries from 90% to 9%.

Warriner thrived at university. Being surrounded by opinionated, intelligent, and ambitious women was exactly the environment that inspired her. Studying Philosophy, Politics and Economics suited her perfectly. She was, most probably from her grandfather, very politically minded. She was also very commercially savvy as well, something which she picked up from a young age looking after her parents' farm.

The years flew by for Warriner and she passed with a First Class Degree, quite an achievement for anyone, let alone a woman at that time. She went on to the London School of Economics as a research scholar, before returning to Oxford for the research fellowship at Somerville College. The rapid change of environment, from a college she knew well and was well known in, to university in the capital, did not faze her in the slightest. In fact, the move to London was her first time living in the city.

From 1933, she lectured on Economics at University College London. It was five years later that she received news she had been granted the chance to travel to the United States of America, via the West Indies to finish her Rockefeller

Fellowship. Just prior to leaving for this trip, she decided her services could be used better elsewhere, namely Czechoslovakia.

CHAPTER 7

THE ARRIVAL OF WARRINER

"Munich had brought disaster to a country well known to me for many years; so at a few days' notice (I decided) to go to Czechoslovakia... to try and help in some way."
Doreen Warriner[35]

The story of how these three individuals came together began on 13th October 1938, when Doreen Warriner's 20-seater airplane touched down on the runway of the brand new Ruzyne Airport in Prague just after midday. She had turned 34 that year.

She headed straight to find her accommodation in the renowned Wenceslas Square, named after the patron saint of Bohemia. The hotel she checked into, The Alcron, was situated just south of the square on Stepanska Street. Apart from her suitcase full of clothes and books, she had with her just over £450 in cash donated by various people and groups in Britain, including £150 from the Save the Children Fund and £20 from Royal Institute of International Affairs.

Shocked and appalled by what she had seen in the news, Warriner felt helpless from the comforts of England, so had decided to head to Prague to offer her services. What these services would be she did not yet know. Warriner envisaged something similar to what she had heard of in Vienna after World War I - working in soup kitchens, cooking meals, and handing out blankets.

With this in mind, the first outing that day from her hotel was to meet with a group of Quakers who had recently set up shop in Prague, called the Society of Friends. The society were intent on supporting the camps in a way that Warriner had envisaged. To her disappointment, she discovered their relief work was yet to commence. Without any significant funds behind them, mixed with a lack of leadership, they had not been able to begin any work. The lady in charge, Mary Penman, explained to Warriner that it was likely to be some weeks until they would need her assistance and for her to return at a later date. Penman had arrived in the country a few months earlier and was a woman of some influence, as the sister of the Labour MP Philip Noel-Baker.

Penman is an important figure in our story as it was her who told Warriner of a group who were more advanced in their support work for the refugee camps and suggested that Warriner visit the man leading this work called Wenzel Jaksch.

Excitedly, that afternoon Warriner headed to Jaksch's flat on Hermannova Street. Knocking on the door, it was answered by a middle-aged man, weak in stature, and on crutches due to a recent car accident. Aged 38, Jaksch was tall, dark-haired and had a small pencil moustache. Living in a flat that belonged to an acquaintance, Jaksch was one of the hundreds of thousands who had fled the Sudetenland. He was, however, in more danger than most, having recently been appointed Chairman of the Sudeten Social Democrats and had been vocally anti-Nazi for many years. Before he left his Sudeten home, arrest warrants had been issued with his name on.

Although he had successfully got to Prague, evading the advancing Nazis soldiers, he was far from safe. For several months Nazi agents had made their way into the city and were now grabbing people at will. Back in 1936, 2,900 suspects "allegedly acting for Germany or Hungary" were arrested by Czech police.[36] But by 1938, the government in Prague were not powerful enough to put a stop to the ever increasing number of agents now embedded in the country and were compelled to turn a blind eye. It was even believed that if anyone was called for by Hitler, the Czech administration would happily hand them over to avoid conflict, and Jaksch knew he would be summoned soon. Furthermore, no-one in the country was naive enough to believe that the Führer would not soon be extending the Nazi rule into the rest of Czechoslovakia. For Jaksch and his many supporters, it was only a matter of time before they were either arrested in the free-land or the free-land would become occupied.

Over a cup of tea that afternoon, Jaksch described the predicament of his party, the SSD, to Warriner. He told her that their only viable option was for the whole group to leave Czechoslovakia together. He explained that to do this he had called in the help of some contacts. Namely, the British Labour Party, the second largest political party in the United Kingdom.

After finishing their tea and Jaksch was staggering to his feet, putting all his weight onto the two crutches, Warriner expressed her desire to help him. He told her that matters were now out of his hands, as the Labour Party had sent two individuals to run operations in Prague. Sensing her disappointment, he suggested Warriner come to a meeting the next day with a colleague of his and these two Brits.

On the morning of 14th October, Warriner travelled to a hotel close to her own, called Steiner Hotel to attend this meeting. Here she was introduced to David Grenfell and William Gillies from the British Labour Party. The former was a formidable character, with very short cut brown hair and a thick moustache that looked like a shadow under his crooked nose. Grenfell came from a poor Welsh family where he had joined his father in the coal mines from the age of 12. He moved abroad a few years later to work in mines in Canada where he also studied evening classes and eventually became an MP in 1922 for the Gower constituency in South Wales. He would soon serve as Secretary for Mines at the Board of Trade under Churchill's coalition government from 1940. It is recorded that Grenfell sat as a delegation member for the London Trade Council with Philip Noel-Baker brother of Mary Penman from the Quaker Movement, although whether he made the connection is not known.

William Gilles, was a larger than life rotund individual, with black hair slicked across his receding forehead and gave Grenfell a run for his money with his moustache, which ran across his top lip and down past his lips to both sides of his chin. At the time, Gillies was International Secretary for the British Labour Party and feared by all in The British Houses of Parliament.

Jaksch had travelled to London at the start of the month to try and drum up support. He was able to use his relationship with Clement Attlee, the Labour Party leader and future Deputy Prime Minister during WWII, who would go on replace Winston Churchill as Prime Minister from 1945 – 1951, to help his cause. Attlee was able to introduce Jaksch to Gillies and Grenfell.

It is not known exactly what was said in their first encounter although Warriner wrote in her diary that both were "horribly rude" and "very difficult to get on with", which gives us an assumption as to how this meeting unfolded. Nevertheless, both sides seemed content to work with each other. Warriner was willing to help and Gillies and

Grenfell were not in a position to turn their moustache framed noses up at such an offer.

For now the team only consisted of only five: the two Labour Party politicians, Warriner, Jaksch and his deputy, Siegfried Taub. As they sat down for their first official meeting, Gillies explained their agenda: to fund and facilitate the evacuation of 100 endangered members of the Sudeten Democratic Party "who had fought against Hitler in the Sudetenland."[37]

Jaksch and Taub as a duet broke in, protesting that given the sheer volume of individuals who were endangered, helping 100 was merely scratching the surface of the problem and almost pointless.

The conversation became heated until Warriner found herself in the middle of a debate. With the British on one side and the Sudetens on the other, she watched as the argument intensified. Like being the spectator at a tennis match, the opinion from one side was served over the table, only to be knocked right back, and so on. The British side was adamant that they would need to choose a select few to get visas, because being overly ambitious with too many requests to the UK's Home Office spelled almost certain failure. From the Sudeten side came the response that they had all fled their homes to be together and that was the way they would stay – whether it be in the safety of London or the danger of Prague.

Eventually, on the evening of 15th October, a ceasefire ensued as the four politicians had reached a stalemate and were tired of debating. That day they had all visited the Passport Control Officer in the British Legation, a man named Harold Gibson. Known to his superiors as Gibby, he was "a small, slight figure with a moustache in proportion."[38] Warriner later wrote that the passport official was "always fully informed" and therefore his word would always be trusted.[39] He told the group he "considered that there was danger to all the Sudeten leaders," reinforcing Jaksch's and Taub's impassioned argument the previous day. It turned out that the reason Gibson was such a reliable source, unbeknown to Warriner, was because he worked for the British Secret Intelligence Service (SIS) commonly known as MI6.

Convinced by Gibson's testimony, the group decided they must compile a list of all the Social Democratic Party members in the camps and then work out who to prioritise for visas. As William Chadwick explained, "Lists were of crucial importance to the refugee process. Everyone had to be on a list in order to apply for a visa. Lists were official. Lists could be taken to government offices and approved by men with rubber stamps sitting behind desks. Lists were important when places were scarce. With luck your name could move up a list and you'd end up on a train or a plane."[40]

Calling a meeting of party leaders and trade union managers, they assembled in Taub's office to start work on their list. Many hours later, as the bell of St. Vitus Cathedral in the centre of Prague chimed midnight, the group were now satisfied they had a complete list of names – pages and pages of them. In total, they had now identified 2,000 people whom they had classed as endangered. Too exhausted to start arguing again as they had done for the past 24 hours, they all knew the list now needed shortening.

So where did they start? Where does anyone start when thousands are in need of help but only a handful can be selected for freedom. How can you decide someone is in more danger than others?

Not deterred, the group began with those who would be regarded as Social Democrat "leaders," and then those heavily associated with and of notable professions, which included teachers, academics, artists and doctors. This still left two thirds of the names still on the list. It was clear to all that this would be far too many visas to obtain. The list was therefore further shortened by the five around a poorly lit kitchen table into the early hours of the morning.

A desolate feeling arose among them as they would reluctantly agree to cross a name off the list, knowing only too well this could be signing that person's death warrant. Eventually, the list consisted of just 250 names. With a sense of hollow achievement, they had reached the lowest possible number. Grenfell and Gillies seemed content, but Warriner thought this to be a wildly optimistic number.

On 16th October, with the finalised list in hand, Gillies and Grenfell rushed back with it to London, leaving Warriner in charge in Prague. Their task back in London was to get as many visas as possible for those they had chosen. Their first visit upon their arrival in Britain was to see Lord Halifax who was serving as Foreign Secretary under Chamberlain's Conservative Government at the time. He had been instrumental in the negotiations of the Munich Agreement and was an ardent supporter of the appeasement strategy. Prepared for some tough negotiations, Gillies and Grenfell were pleasantly surprised when Halifax approved the visa request for 250 individuals without hesitation or protest. Either the barriers of British politics lowered temporarily or Halifax dared not get into an argument with two such formidable members of his opposition.

They had overcome a major obstacle, but they were immediately confronted by another: Money. One of the conditions for an entry visa to Britain was a £50 guarantee for each. Gillies and Grenfell decided that they, the British Labour Party, would be financial guarantors for all 250 visas. Of course, they never got this approved by the party's treasurer nor checked the party were happy to spend their funds in this manner.

Back in Prague, Jakch, Taub, and Warriner had their own hurdles to jump. Most importantly, what form of transport they should use to take these people. The answer to this would shape other obstacles. For travelling by air was the easiest, as it only needed an entry visa into Britain, whereas travelling by train across Poland, then by boat to Britain, meant they were also required to carry a travel permit by the Polish authorities. To Warriner, planes seemed the best option and much less hassle than going by land, until they discovered how much it would cost. When she heard the price, she quickly decided that trains might actually not be as much hassle. Outside the financial benefits, trains were far larger than any airplane available, meaning much fewer journeys would be required. The issue they faced was that the Czech railway system "had been grossly mutilated by the annexations" they had been dealt after the Munich Conference.[41]

Seeking help from a Czech Travel Agency, Čedok which still services over 300,000 tourists to this day, Warriner was pointed in the direction of the large refugee-designated trains. However, having discussed this option with Jaksch and Taub, they agreed it would be too risky, as it was an easy target for Nazi agents.

Half their time was spent rushing between different travel company's offices and the other half they would spend in Jaksch's flat buried in paperwork. Each person on the list needed to provide them with their passport, which Warriner in turn would take to the British Consul where it would be cross referenced with the approved names by Lord Halifax's staff in London. Each passport needed approving and stamping one by one – a time-consuming and arduous task.

They then needed to be taken to the Prague Consulate, whose disobliging, painfully slow and disorganised staff would then be issue a travel visa.

Two days after Grenfell and Gillies had returned to London, all 250 from their list were now approved to travel. They all had a British visa issued by the Home Office, a travel permit through Poland approved by the Polish Consul and a £50 guarantee paid for by the Labour Party. What they did not have was a mode of transport to actually use all these gifts.

On 19th October, Grenfell returned to Prague to help organise some sort of transport. By the time he landed in Czechoslovakia he had decided and without discussing with the others, that the safest option would be to take a select group with him to find their own way to Poland.

CHAPTER 8

THE FIRST RESCUES

"I would not have been here if it had not been for (Grenfell)"
Ernest Neuschel[42]

Dusk had come and gone and now Prague was thrown into complete darkness. It was the night of 23rd October when Grenfell set off on an unknown voyage to a destination he had not yet discovered with 50 of the 250 men from the list.

Arriving at Wilson Station late that evening, Warriner and the wives and children of the 50 men said their goodbyes and parted company. The many emotions floating around consisted mainly of uncertainty and fear. It usually goes against all their human instincts for men to leave a sinking ship with their loved ones still on deck. The men did genuinely believe that by vacating the area they would ensure the safety of their wives and children – they were jumping overboard to stop the ship from sinking.

As the train strained its way out of the station, Warriner and the lonely women and children headed back through the cold streets to their dwellings with no idea of the fate of their husbands.

It was not until another day had past, on the evening of 24th October, that Warriner received a call for Grenfell to tell her their first mission had been a success. Travelling by slow night train, it took 30 hours for him and his 50 men to travel the 300 miles to Poland, but they had arrived safely, albeit exhausted. Without any time to lose, Warriner went back to the list and chose another 20 men to take. They had agreed they should get as many men to Poland as possible, before embarking on a ferry crossing, which were already very infrequent.

Despite having caught the flu, Warriner and her 20 men set off on 25th October to take the same expedition their colleagues had a couple of nights before. Similar to the previous scene, a line of trembling women and children formed a solemn line along the platform, watching the men of their households disappear into the darkness.

It was an incredibly long and tedious journey, heading through the depths of Slovakia by night steam train, before changing to a motor train to pass through the ruins of Orava Castle, Oravský Podzámok, up into the Slovakian mountains. They arrived in the northern village of Suchá Hora, where there was a tiny frontier post, bordering Poland. Disembarking from the motor train, they had a long wait for the whole of 26th October, lying in the sun and eating eggs from the local inn (the only food for sale). It was not until night fell that their connecting train arrived on the Polish side of the border.

They then endured their first border crossing, with endless questioning, passport checking and bag searching. Nevertheless, they all made it across without any real drama, into the safety of Poland. Back on another train, they were slowly rattling towards the southern Polish town of Nowy Targ, which, unbeknownst to anyone, would be invaded by the Nazi war machine under a year later and become a major Jewish ghetto.

Once in Nowy Targ, having missed their connecting train due to the border delays earlier that day, Warriner went on to Krakow by the "special tornado express" alone, given the expense of travelling in such luxury, to meet the waiting Grenfell. Meanwhile in Nowy Targ, the 20 men remained, shivering from the cold and fatigue, drinking vodka to keep warm and to calm their nerves, before catching the midnight train to Krakow.

Grenfell greeted Warriner with a gift and some words. The gift: a plane ticket from Warsaw back to Prague. The words: "Go back and get some more."[43] He hoped that she would be able to get back to Prague in time to bring another group to catch the same ferry as the 70 now congregated in Poland. The most reliable was the British liner, which made the voyage fortnightly.

Early on 27th October, Warriner was back on a train, hurtling towards Warsaw, where she rushed to catch the 7 a.m. plane to Prague. Two days after first leaving, five trains, three countries and very little sleep, she arrived back in Prague only to do the same again.

As Warriner endured her gruelling journey back to Czechoslovakia, Grenfell discovered there would not be time to get another group out on the same boat. The British liner was due to leave the next day. He got word to Warriner's hotel and took both groups now consisting of 70 men to Gdynia, the northern seaport of Gdańsk Bay on the south coast of the Baltic Sea. Here, he arranged for them to travel by sea the remainder of the journey. And off they went – 70 persecuted men who were earmarked by Hitler, to the safety of Britain where they would be able to seek asylum.

Back in Prague, Warriner was relieved to have a note from Grenfell telling her the next voyage was be postponed. From her hotel on Stepanska Street, she spent the next few days working through the mountain of paperwork she had accumulated, trying to come up with a more manageable system. This was bothering her, but not as much as another worry she had. Funding was still a challenge – the team were aware they could not support the operation from the Labour Party funds alone, who were none the wiser of the previous two voyages costing them £3,500, but would surely become suspicious if it continued.

In the event of this happening, the British politicians were focused on finding funding from elsewhere. On the 31st October, Grenfell returned to Prague by plane. He had arranged for him and Warriner to meet with Sir Ronald Macleay, formerly the counsellor of British Legation in Prague and now chairman of the Lord Mayor's Committee for Czech Refugees. At the age of 68, Macleay had served as Counsellor for the British Legation in Peking (now Beijing) during the Great War and then later ambassador to China until 1922.

Macleay was in part responsible for the swift response to the Sudeten crisis, although his focus was solely on those with a

Czech background. Grenfell hoped they would be able to negotiate for the German group now under his watch to be included in the Lord Mayor's Committee for Czech Refugees. It was not the case and the meeting turned out to be brief and abrupt. After only a few sentences into their pitch, Warriner and Grenfell were interrupted by Macleay simply quoting the Nazi stance on the refugee crisis, stating "these men are Germans... in the spirit of the Munich Agreement they must go back to Germany."[44]

As a lifelong Tory supporter, it is little surprise that Macleay was less than receptive by an approach from the Labour Party, asking for him to assist their Socialist companions. During his time in China, he was described by his American counterpart as someone who did not imagine "good could come out of any liberal ideas."[45]

After what turned out to be a very brief and unsuccessful visit, Grenfell returned to London in the desperate hope of finding funds. For the time being, they would continue to rely on the Labour Party funding, with the realisation that this could stop at any point. His trip was not completely wasted, as there was just enough time for him to spend with Warriner, discussing the logistics of the up-and-coming voyages for the remaining 180 men on their list. The plan had been for Warriner to accompany all journeys to Warsaw, to ensure safe passage. They agreed that this was an ineffective use of her time, which would be better spent focusing on the administration in Prague.

Grenfell suggested they seek someone to act as the courier for future journeys. They decided on Tessa Rowntree, a lady working for the Quaker movement, because Grenfell said, "she looks like a tough girl."[46] She was indeed tough, but also very brave and delighted to be able to help.

On 2nd November Rowntree took the next group on the same route as the past two journeys to Poland. Despite getting stuck by the border for some time, they crossed and headed north. Rowntree waited for the next group. This was recorded in her cousin, Jean Rowntree's obituary, "When Jean Rowntree arrived... Tessa Rowntree was leading a convoy of refugees to the Russian and Polish borders."[47]

The next two journeys were done by Alec Dickson, found by the News Chronicle before the arrival of John Ingman, who was sent by the request of the Workers' Travel Association and would act as the regular courier for the remainder of the operation. Through this story his incredible bravery and integrity is astonishing.

By 9th November, just 17 days after the first voyage began, nearly all the 250 from the list were settled safely in Britain, or heading through Poland on their way to Britain. It would seem apt for a time of celebration as their mission had been a success. But for Warriner, no such festivities were in mind. She realised that they had only scratched the surface of the crisis and "the real nature of the refugee problem (she) had not realised at all."[48]

CHAPTER 9

THE BRITISH COMMITTEE FOR REFUGEES IN CZECHOSLOVAKIA

"A refugee is I, you or they if circumstances decree it. It is a survival which is unglamorous, often sordid, and has to be made the best of. It is a state to shake off as quickly as possible."
Unknown WWII Refugee[49]

It was true that by the second week of November 1938, the 250 most vulnerable men of the Sudeten German Party had now been evacuated to the safety of Britain. However, left in their wake was a scene of devastation. Without the support from their husbands and fathers, both physical and financial, the women and children left behind were struggling to survive. Yet, their welfare was still lower down on the priorities of Warriner, Jaksch, Taub and the two British Labour politicians, who were now focused on the men who had not made it onto the list of 250 in Jaksch's kitchen on 15th October.

Gillies and Grenfell believed they could gain further visas from Lord Halifax, which had turned out to be much more straightforward than either of them could have imagined. Where they knew they had a problem was with funding. It is not known what the reaction was to their allocation of Labour Party funds to all previous rescues, or indeed if this had even been discovered by this point.

Gillies and Grenfell appealed to their colleagues within the British Parliament, no matter which side of the House they sat, for a more robust solution. Grenfell ended up joining the Parliamentary Committee on Refugees as Vice-Chairman, along with politician Arthur Salter at the same level. The committee was led by Conservative Victor Cazalet and had Eleanor Rathbone, the independent MP as Honorary Secretary. They described themselves as "concerned not with individual refugees, whose cases are dealt with by the appropriate voluntary organisations, but with the general problems of the refugee question as a whole."[50] Over the months, they slowly built up cross-party support for their cause. Lobbying in Parliament for the cause of all refugees, they appointed someone to spearhead operations in Czechoslovakia.

Sir Walter Layton visited Prague towards the end of November 1938 to see the situation for himself. Layton was a successful economist and businessman, who had been editor of The Economist from 1922 until that year, when he was called upon by the government. Having worked for the Ministry of Munitions throughout World War I, during the next World War he was given roles within the Ministry of Supply and the Ministry of Production, before being appointed Head of Joint War Production Staff in 1942.

A man of considerable influence and stature, Layton had been selected by parliamentary members to lead all refugee issues related to Czechoslovakia. Sir Walter was a tall, austere man, with a long nose and was always impeccably well dressed; never being caught without a fine tailored three-piece suit and gold pocket watch. The father of seven children, he was a formidable and commanding figure. On his whistle stop tour of the Czech capital, he visited aid organisation after aid organisation, seeing for himself the success, or not, they were having. All these charity groups were working towards the same goal, but they were all going about it completely differently.

He became only too aware that it would be counterproductive to have so many well-meaning groups trying to resolve a crisis of this scale, each with their own agenda. Layton decided the only way to move forward to any real form of success was to have one consolidated British effort. He therefore created The British Committee for Refugees from Czechoslovakia (BCRC). The function of the BCRC role was to use "the funds collected from both the British public and the Government to assist Sudeten Germans, Reich Germans and Austrians to leave Czech territory and reach Britain, on the condition that they arrived as trans migrants bound for resettlement elsewhere in the British Empire."[51]

This government supported, non-sectarian organisation comprised of and was funded by three key areas: The Labour Party, The News Chronicle and the Quakers, all of whom were already working in the country. After some debate with Layton, each organisation reluctantly realised their full potential and effectiveness when working together.

He now needed a first rate efficient team. With Sir Walter as the creator, he selected his sister, Margaret Layton, to be secretary of the BCRC based out of London. Equally forbidding as her brother, Sir Walter knew his sibling would be the perfect match to any bureaucratic obstacles that might arise. He asked a senior and well-regarded figure in the Labour Party, Ewart Gladstone Culpin to be Chairman of the BCRC. Culpin was a seasoned politician who had spent nearly 15 years as a Labour Party Alderman for the London County Council, before being made Chairman of the Council that year.

Layton then turned his lens to who should be the lead from within Prague. There were two obvious choices, Mary Penman from the Quakers and David Wills from the News Chronicle fund. There was also a wild card – the young maverick Warriner, who in comparison was vastly less experienced or qualified for such a task.

On his visit, in part to make this appointment, he was incredibly impressed by Warriner. He was struck by her drive, determination and bravery, all of which she had demonstrated during her journey across Poland. With her current makeshift team of politicians and couriers, she was the only one to have any successful rescue operations to her name, even though her resume had no mention of having done any humanitarian work on it prior to her visit to Prague that year.

Despite her very limited track record of running such a scheme elsewhere, Warriner was asked by Layton to be the official representative in Prague. He was taking a considerable risk; one which he would regret at times, but overall was the turning point for those in danger in the country. His decision to appoint her lead to one of the most successful rescue missions in modern times.

The role gave Warriner complete autonomy to run all Prague based operations. Along with a requisitioned office on Voršilská Street, an official title, secretarial support and headed notepaper, she was given full control of the News Chronicle Fund, which was valued around £7,000, today worth just under £333,000. Up to this point David Wills, who was returning to London, controlled the fund. The four women assigned to support Warriner from an administration perspective were Hilde Patz, Christine Maxwell, Alois Mollik, and Margaret Dougan.

With a functioning team now in place the BCRC's official strategy was simple: To assist the welfare of political refugees and those who had opposed the rise of Hitler, now known as the "old Reich refugees." The BCRC believed that ultimately these people would only be safe if they were to leave the country.

The organisation's priority was therefore to evacuate as many endangered individuals as possible before the inevitable arrival of Hitler and support them with accommodation upon their arrival into Britain. Despite having full control over the News Chronicle Fund, Warriner was instructed that it be used to provide immediate relief and essential supplies to those in camps and should not be absorbed with any other capital used to aid people's travel out of the country or to be used as a financial guarantee for any refugees to travel to Britain. It is not clear exactly where this order came from or the precise science behind such a request.

Nevertheless, Warriner respected it fully and only gave the money out for urgent requests by homeless families. For Gillies and Grenfell back in Britain, they were still burdened by the prospect of raising enough money to sponsor those due to arrive in the country. It was something the Foreign Office would not budge on and became the most pressing matter for them. Along with the Layton siblings, Cuplin and many others, the British side of the BCRC set about writing articles and letters in the papers, calling in favours from their long list of influential friends and doing all they could to raise cash.

Warriner was in complete control of all aspects across the sea in Prague, leaving the others to focus on purely on funding. Having arrived in the city only five weeks previously, Warriner had advanced from an amateur aid-worker to the helm of a fully funded humanitarian organisation. Immediately, she set about to arrange for more members of the Jakcsh and Taub's party to leave the country.

The key to any success would be the relationship between the BCRC and the British Legation. It was around this time, 6th November 1938 that the British Government sent the young Irishman in his early forties, Robert Stopford, to act as Liaison Officer in the Legation. According to the announcement of his appointment in the British newspaper Western Daily Press his remit was "to keep the British Government informed about the progress" of aid in the country.[52] Stopford was an exceptional Civil Servant, who was able to work closely with the Czech Government and later with the Nazis. His influence, stature and intelligence earned him huge respect and was instrumental to Warriner's work. It cannot be underestimated how important it was having him on side and his arrival signalled success for future rescue work.

***

Warriner had only been in her newly appointed position as head of the Prague office of the BCRC for a few days, with barely enough time to settle into her newly requisitioned office or have her calling cards printed, when her mission was nearly forced to an abrupt halt.

It was on 27th November that she had a list, numbering close to 150, consisting of the wives and children of some of those who had already left as well as further endangered men, all with visas to enter Britain on trains to depart from Wilson Station on 6th December, when the Polish Consul in Prague suddenly refused any transit visas through Poland, claiming it was a direct instruction from Warsaw. As this was the only proven way for the refugees to travel, this caused Warriner great concern and if not resolved, could jeopardise all future transports. The thought of using another route, like travelling through Germany, was far too risky for the BCRC. Until this point, the Poles had not had an issue with any refugee transits, especially as Warriner and her team were able to show that everyone travelling had a British visa and would therefore have no intension or incentive to want to remain in Poland. Britain was one of the safest places to be in Europe, far more so than Poland.

Jakchs and Taub told Warriner this was politically motivated, believing the Nazis were exerting pressure on the

Polish government. She was suspicious of this theory and found it hard to believe, given the wider political picture of Europe. Similar to the Sudetenland, the Polish region of Zaolzie had been awarded to Czechoslovakia by the Red Army in 1920, causing much unrest within the Poland. The rise of the Third Reich gave Poland the chance to reclaim their land from a weakened Czech neighbour and earlier in October 1938 Zaolzie was handed back to the Polish. Immediately, the Polish government "began to remove Czechs and Germans from their jobs," aiming to deport of as many as possible.[53] Warriner questioned, therefore, why they would want to stop Czechs and Germans leaving Czechoslovakia and heading for Britain.

Her suspicions were confirmed on 6th December when the Consul in Prague said, "You can receive visas for 12th December, provided that the transport travels by Gdynia-America line."[54]

Warriner correctly suspected that Gdynia-America, a Polish shipping line and the Consul were working together in order to line their own pockets. With such a high demand for transport, the travel company wanted a slice of the action. This would not have been a major issue if the Gdynia-America line was not so unreliable and infrequent. The British line, which Grenfell had now personally tried and tested, ran fortnightly and without delay, meaning there was little risk of the refugees being stranded for any significant length of time in Poland at the port of Gdynia.

Outraged, Warriner booked her travel and flew straight to Warsaw the next day, 7th December, to meet a representative from the British Embassy in Poland. Gillies arranged for her to see Robin Hankey, the former Private Secretary to British

Foreign Secretary and future Prime Minister, Anthony Eden. Hankey, having been briefed by Gillies, immediately took Warriner to the Polish Foreign Office to confront them on this issue. The son of a former Cabinet Secretary, he was a man of considerable influence and superior intellect, proficient in German, French, Italian, Polish, Romanian, Persian, and Arabic.

Slightly intimidated by the force of Hankey, with Warriner at his side, the Polish officials assured them that transit visas would continue to be issued and that there was no such provision in place for the use of Gdynia-America. Given Hankey's close ties to the British political elite, the local authorities were eager to keep him, and their British allies, onside. This would turn out to benefit the Polish government, as Hankey was "one of the first to learn of Hitler's invasion of Poland," [55] helping the escape of President Władysław Raczkiewicz and Prime Minister General Władysław Sikorski to form the Polish Government in Exile.

Victorious, on 8th December, Warriner flew back to Prague to confront the Consul and present her findings. She discovered that in her absence, he was trying to intimidate one of Warriner's secretaries, Hilde Patz, to agree to the exclusive use of Gdynia-America. Luckily Patz was as much a force as Warriner and flatly declined to agree to anything, despite some quite heated words thrown in her direction. The Consul refused to believe that Warriner had just returned from the Foreign Office in Warsaw and telephoned them directly from Patz's desk, where he was told Warriner was not bluffing and had indeed rumbled him. He reluctantly agreed to allow the travel visas she required without condition.

The Consul was not quite finished with his attempts to disrupt Warriner's mission, and was livid that she had exposed his money-making scheme. On 14th December the paperwork for 150 next in line to travel arrived, some of whom had husbands now safe in Britain. However, Warriner noticed that the passports were stamped with new wording threatening that they had the right to be refused entry to Poland at the frontier.

She decided that the safest way to ensure the success of their trip was for her to go with them. Dropping everything, Warriner set off on the 11 p.m. train to Ostrava, heading past two strips of Nazi-occupied territory in Austria lined with floodlit swastikas. They passed over the frontier with even less trouble than her first voyage six weeks prior, and the group of 150 headed on to Gdynia under the leadership of the trustworthy John Ingman, while Warriner returned to Prague. They were then able to board their British fortnightly ferry and head to the shores of England.

Clearly, as she had expected all along, there was an attempted scam some Čedok employees, Gdynia-America shipping and the Polish authorities in order to share the profits. As William Chadwick points out, despite this being a difficult and worrying experience for Warriner, it "would stand her in good stead later when she indulged in a few underground railway manoeuvres of her own."[56]

Back in London, Layton heard of this mini victory, knowing only too well that he had made exactly the right decision to appoint Warriner. She now had 220 rescues to her name, although what followed made him question this thought.

Layton was one of many visitors to Prague, with large numbers of well-wishers arriving to look around the camps and generally offer their support. This was gradually grinding on the gears of Warriner. Wealthy individuals and politicians were flying into the country simply with the intention of giving relief. This would usually be in the guise of wool and chocolate. Most would ignore the calls by the BCRC for donations to fund visas and travel logistics. Many thought that short-term relief to the camps was the solution.

Barely any of those who had a whistle-stop trip to the city saw the true devastation within the camps. Warriner remarked that if they had, they would know that "it was emigration rather than relief that was needed, visas not chocolate."[57] Not one to hold back, Warriner called upon the media for support.

Writing to The Telegraph on 9th December and The Manchester Guardian the following day, she talked of the growing corruption within refugee camps, which were already overcrowded and under resourced. In what turned out to be counterproductive and in many ways, offensive, she turned on those who had provided donations claiming their ignorance, "There is some confusion in Great Britain about the real state of affairs" in Prague," going on to say that those who were donating were simply doing so to clear "one's own conscience."[58]

To say that this letter caused some upset is an understatement. Gillies was enraged, simply sending a telegram to Warriner saying "no more pronouncements" which seemed to aggravate her even more. However, it was the chairman if the BCRC, Culpin, who was seriously angered by her words, claiming that it would cost the organisation over £100,000 in donations. He wrote to her saying how the letter had "made much trouble" and following with the chilling words every school child of the time would have shivered at, "I'll see you in my study" when she was in the UK on a pre-planned trip.[59]

Despite their anger at this indescribable lack of tact, it was in fact Culpin and Gillies who ignored calls for Warriner to be sacked over her comments. They realised that it was out of frustration towards the governments of Czechoslovakia and Britain rather than aimed at those who were genuinely trying to help. Nevertheless, it shows that Warriner was not the veteran people made her out to be and exposed her serious naivety of public relations. This letter would go on to seriously jeopardise any further transports from Prague until alternative funding could be found. For Warriner, there was no ill intent, purely a lack of judgement. She later explained that she "felt bound to say something on behalf of the people who could not."[60]

It is true that Cuplin and Gillies knew only too well the lack of support for Czechoslovakia. By July 1938, over 150,000 Jews and the politically endangered from Germany and Austria had been granted asylum in Britain, Palestine, Brazil, Bolivia, France, Belgium, Scandinavia, and the United States. But only a fraction from Czechoslovakia, nearly all of whom had been able to go through personal wealthy connections or the help of the BCRC.

Warriner herself flew to London on 21st December, in the hope of persuading the authorities to deliver faster visas. While in Britain, she received several dressing downs from Gillies, Cuplin and Layton. However, she had not flown back to listen to people's negative opinions – she had flown back to obtain a further 200 visas. There was just enough money left in her funds to evacuate this whole group. In Warriner's mind, she still stood by the letter she had written despite the backlash the organisation had received. The BCRC were relying heavily on donations and volunteers of any size. This letter doubtlessly turned many people away. Luckily, there was one man who not deterred. Martin Blake had seen the appeals from the BCRC, thrown his hat into the ring and planned to drop everything to fly to Prague to help. Quite the opposite to being offended by Warriner's letter, he agreed completely. Being the Eve of Christmas, he was unable to leave for a few days.

Warriner returned from a damp and frosty Britain on 23rd December, having got stuck in Paris due to fog, arriving in an icy and snowy Prague late on Christmas Eve.

CHAPTER 10

THE CHILDREN'S SECTION

"By the time war was declared on 3ʳᵈ September 1939,
almost 10,000 children (had been recused) directly from
Austria and Germany. But what about the threatened
children in Czechoslovakia?"
Vera Gissing & Muriel Emanuel[61]

The following day Warinner visited one of the refugee camps, explaining, "On Christmas morning I went round to see the children in the Y.W.C.A and the home, with presents, and there heard of the diphtheria epidemic in Dolni Krup, in which four children had died."[62] Such was the epidemic, that Czech authorities forbade anyone from visiting the camps in fear of it spreading further.

Quietly walking the streets of Prague that evening, Warriner was at one with her thoughts. Putting aside the squabbles she was having with her counterparts in London, she had always had her mind focused on one task: saving the politically persecuted and now their families. Although she had seen tremendous results in doing so, she was now witnessing the sheer devastation that was left behind. By this point, some 250 people had been swiftly, seamlessly and effectively whisked out of the danger Hitler posed, but in their wake, were literally thousands of vulnerable people left behind. Without the necessary funding and with the sheer amount of time it took to get just one person the necessary paperwork to leave, Warriner felt completely helpless. What was even scarier for her, was with such a huge number of displaced people strewn around the city, a crisis of abandoned children was emerging. The past month had proven such a struggle to focus on one group, she was realistic enough to know she could not save them all.

Then arrived the young, intelligent and passionate Martin Blake. Blake was taking some time out from teaching at Westminster School and was in fact supposed to be accompanying pupils on a skiing trip. Inspired by Warriner's letter, he scrapped this and headed for Prague. Although it is not officially noted, he immediately began working directly for Warriner from her Voršilská Street office. Warriner herself had only just returned to Prague after her trip to London, when she was greeted by a fresh-faced Englishman offering his assistance.

Blake was set to work alongside other volunteers, including Bill Barazetti, a refugee himself. So entrenched in these long days, trying to grapple with such a hopeless situation, it only dawned on Blake a few days later that had never told his friend of the drastic change of holiday plan and destination.

Meanwhile, back on the snowy shores of Britain in late December 1938, the young 29-year-old stockbroker, Nicolas Winton, was packing his skis and winter clothing, preparing for a trip to the Alps with his close friend Martin. While choosing which set of goggles to take, blissfully unaware of any change to the schedule, Winton received a phone call from Blake saying, "I've cancelled the skiing trip and I am calling from Prague. Forget the skis and join me immediately... I have something much more interesting than skiing for you here."[63]

With cautious intrigue, Winton switched his ski outfit with a thick woollen suit, re-packed his bag and headed for the airport.

On New Year's Eve, as the British prepared to celebrate the arrival of 1939, Winton was arriving at Prague. He headed for Hotel Šroubek in Wenceslas Square, checked in to room 171 to drop his luggage off before meeting Blake in the lobby. It was not until March 1998 that Winton ever went back to this hotel, now named Hotel Europa. Upon his return, despite it being 59 years after he was last there he remarked that the room was nearly exactly the same, saying "yes, yes, I do recognise it!"[64] The remarkably similar suite would become home for Winton over his three-week stay as well as also doubling up as an office. There were two rooms, one for sleeping and one for working. It was in this makeshift office that Winton would go on to run his part in the rescue. The rooms were well decorated with fresh wallpaper, oak panelled flooring, and sparsely laid out furniture.

Blake wasted no time filling Winton in on the refugee situation, which he had now seen first-hand. Winton had heard a lot of what had been happening in the country, but in the short 10-minute walk from his hotel to the BCRC offices, Blake was able to give him a much more frank description than that appearing in the news.

Arriving at the small side street, just past the National Theatre, they entered the recently dedicated offices for all rescue operations. Having to push through a huge number of poorly clothed, cold and dishevelled cadaver-thin men, women and children lining the corridors, Winton met Warriner for the first time and was instantly drawn to her. He was in awe of what she had managed to achieve and wasted no time in offering his assistance.

His first day involved supporting two of Warriner's staff, to meet with the queues of people wanting to see them for help. Winton quickly noticed the number of mothers who would turn up, desperate for some support, which the BCRC could only provide in the guise of small sums of money for much needed food and shelter.

That evening, back at his hotel for some dinner with Blake, they discussed his first day. What was apparent to them both was that simply helping Warriner with what she was already doing would have less impact than focusing on a group she had no time to prioritise: The children. She had made her concerns known to Blake around the children situation which was rapidly unfolding. That evening, the two of them set the wheels in motion for what would be one the most famous and celebrated humanitarian act to come out of World War II.

The next morning, Winton had made up his mind and had decided to dedicate himself to the children exclusively. With Blake, he presented the idea to Warriner as she arrived in her office that morning. She was only too delighted to hand him full autonomy of running the newly formed and unofficial Children's Section of the BCRC. He recalled in a letter to his mother that "Miss Warriner has already asked me to be Secretary of a Children's Committee for Czechoslovakia which I suggested should be formed."[65]

Knowing he needed more time, Winton immediately wrote to Mr Hart, his boss at Crews & Company, to ask for an extension to his holiday by one week. Even prolonging his trip to three weeks would be an insufficient amount of time to organise something of this magnitude. He would also be without the support of Blake, who had to return to England for the start of the spring term at school.

He voiced his concern to Warriner, who also wrote to Hart asking for Winton to remain in Prague for longer. The way she describes him and the language she uses in this letter shows the value she placed on Winton after knowing him for a relatively short amount of time, "Mr Winton is, as you know, working with the refugee organisations here and has taken over the organisation of the child emigration. This is now at a very critical point and if he leaves at the moment, I am afraid the whole thing would come to a standstill. Could he not possibly remain (longer)? I am relying on him to organise the chaos which exists here and then to bring the documents to London. I am very shorthanded and have no one else who can take over the work is doing. It really is essential if the plans are to go through... (Winton's) energy is absolutely invaluable and he had drawn all the different organisations together in a most amazing way and brought order into the chaos."[66]

On 9th January Winton received a rather abrupt letter back, stating that although his boss was aware of his "heroic work" for the "thousands of poor devils who are suffering through no fault of their own" he would rather Winton returned to work after the two agreed weeks.[67] He made the point that money was to be made from the Economic uncertainty in Europe and he needed his whole team assembled as soon as possible to maximise on this. To his dismay, Winton rebelled against his boss and remained in Prague for a further ten days.

Due to the changing political landscape in Europe and in part to the letter Warriner had written before Christmas, the BCRC were struggling to fund any future transports out of Prague. This allowed Winton a significant amount of time to spend with Warriner, taking her council regularly. Although she provided well needed advice, she had little knowledge of the legal or practical aspects of unaccompanied infants leaving the country.

Therefore Winton turned to the person he was closest to – his mother. Throughout his time in Prague, he continually wrote to his mother, usually on a daily basis. On this occasion he asked for assistance, "Could you go to the Immigration Section of the Home Office and find out what guarantees you need to bring a child into the country?" In this letter, he asks several questions, including, "If a family wishes to guarantee for a child, what do they have to do?" And, "Can one get a child over if someone guarantees for a year? If not can one if the guarantee is for two years? What is the shortest guarantee required?"

These questions clearly show the inexperience of the newly formed Children's Section of the BCRC. These questions relate to the logistics of granting children refugee status in Britain.

Where Warriner's expertise was essential was advising on the best way to get children to the point of being able to leave Prague. She told Winton the most important thing she had learnt when she had first arrived in the city – create lists. She explained to him that the key to any of the successful escape missions she had pioneered was to first understand who needed to escape, how many and most importantly, who should get priority.

He therefore turned to the aid organisations who already had large numbers of endangered children on their books. There were five main groups: Jews, Catholics, Communists, Austrians, and political writers. These organisations had not had the foresight of Layton to consolidate into one entity and were subsequently very ineffective. They seemed to Winton to be actively in competition with each other, like political parties pushing for the spotlight.

Immediately after being contacted by Winton, each group understandably wanted the BCRC's newly formed Children's Section to prioritise their 'clients' (the infants they took responsibility for). Winton asked them to provide as much detail as possible on the children they represented, with the very least, sending over a list of names to give him an idea of numbers. What bemused him was that all five groups responded in the same way – they refused to be the first to share such details, as they were convinced that Winton would send this on to one of their 'competitors' and therefore become irrelevant. Such was the toxic politics which surrounded this humanitarian disaster.

Winton used his experience from his business background, applying a simple but clever strategy. He simply wrote to each organisation, telling them that he had "a list from another group and would be using that unless they sent theirs immediately."[68] This was complete fiction on Winton's part and he had no such document by this point. Needless to say, within days the five organisations sent over the information he needed. Winton was now in possession of the details of 760 children. However, details ranged from full copy of passport, school results, and photographs, to simply a child's name which was illegible to the human eye.

He set about organising the list in order of most detail to least. For those he did not have enough suitable information on, he would request more or an audience with the parents. Using the Hotel Šroubek on Wenceslas Square as the headquarters for the BCRC's Children's Section, families were told to report to room 171 as soon as they could to discuss the potential evacuation of their children.

Queues of dishevelled families became a regular fixture down the corridor of Winton's hotel floor. Nevertheless, he would see each family individually, taking down details of their children which would include age, hobbies and would take photographs. Winton would be bombarded by literally hundreds of questions from worried parents, usually asking, "How long will it be before my child can go?" and, "Will I soon be able to follow my child?"[69]

Not only was this a draining and time consuming activity, the difficulty of the task was only exacerbated by the fact that Winton knew not a word of Czech. He spoke German fluently, but as this was the language of the enemy he found that people would immediately refuse to engage in conversation with him. Each time a trembling parent would enter the office of the man they had been told was helping children to escape, they were alarmed to be spoken to in the language of their nemesis. Many adults thought they were being tricked by Nazi agents. So began a rushed master class in basic Czech from some of Warriner's native team. It is fair to say that Winton failed to grasp the basics of the language, and therefore settled on one phase in Czech, "I am British, but I cannot speak Czech," which seemed to do the trick.[70]

The language barrier was not only an issue when communicating with those he was trying to aid. During his first week in the city, after what had been a busy day of meetings and visits, Winton went for a walk on the streets. He intended to peacefully organise his thoughts, when he stumbled upon a group of youths marching and chanting. For Winton, any level of excitement was good enough, so he decided to join in with these individuals, with no clue as to what they were marching for and what they were chanting. As the procession of passionate protesters advanced towards the city centre, the energy levels increased as did the volume of their chants. In time the men and women cried *"Židé jsou naše neštěstí"*(Jews are our misfortune) over and over. Winton detected the tone of the men and women around him become menacing as their faces slowly turned more purple. He became alarmed as the shouts turned into fullblown screaming, nevertheless, he tried to match the tempo and volume as best he could.

Soon, the police arrived in force. What followed was a shouting match, with the police and protesters barking at each other like angry dogs. Winton decided that this was the opportune time for him to retire from his brief career as a protester, although he was still unaware what he was protesting for or against. Back in his hotel, Winton discovered from a member of staff that this was in fact an anti-Jewish march. The phase being chanted was "the Jews are our misfortune," a well-known saying coined from Der Stürmer, the tabloid Nazi propaganda newspaper. Winton wrote to his mother that night, "I must confess to having taken part in an anti-Jewish demonstration," despite being of Jewish origin.[71]

His routine from the offset became incredibly intense. Throughout the daytime, he would be out visiting camps, meeting and interviewing parents and children, trying to gather as much data as possible. People began knocking on his hotel door in the early morning hours, often before 6 a.m., which he would answer with a white beard of shaving foam on his face. Everyone wanted to know whether he could get their children to safety. By this point, many parents reluctantly comprehended that it would be impossible for their whole family to escape, but did not accept the same for their children. They had to compromise by sending their children away, with a fading hope that they would be able to follow at some point in the future. Winton wrote to his mother that he knew that for the mothers he had met, "circumstances will prevent (them) ever seeing (their) child again."[72]

Winton had now been in the country for 10 days. In this short space of time, he had met hundreds of families wanting his help, visited various aid organisations, mastered a phrase of the local language and accidentally become an anti-Semitic protester. However, he had not witnessed any form of rescue, something Warriner had seen from the very start of her time in Prague which had motivated her to achieve what she had. She had complete approbation and faith in Winton's ambition, drive and dedication, but feared he might become disengaged when he returned to London. So she organised for him to witness a rescue in person. On 12th January Winton accompanied, purely as a logistical aid, a group of 20 Jewish children to the airport, who were about to embark on a flight to London. Photos of him with the children would go on to be shared worldwide many years later.

The trip was being funded and organised by The Barbican Mission, whose primary purpose was to convert Jews to Christianity. Demonstrating the desperation of Jewish parents, they were willing to turn their children away from their own faith, in order to guarantee their safety. The following day, the New York Times reported that "the children will be brought up in London homes and in the Barbican Mission until they are 18 years old, when, after training as artisans, they will be sent to British colonies and dominions."[73]

In Winton's mind, this was Christian blackmail, used against vulnerable people who were simply looking to secure the safety of their children. His view on religion was, "If you believe in God, then I do not understand what difference it makes if you believe as a Christian, a Jew, a Buddhist, or a Muslim. The fundamentals of all religions are basically the same: goodness, love, not to kill, and to look after your parents and those close to you. I believe people should think less about the aspects of religion that divide them and more about what these beliefs have in common, which is ethics."[74] In the months that followed, Winton would often come up against similar religious obstacles.

CHAPTER 11

THE CAMPS

"They were unheated, food was rationed, blankets were scarce,
broken windows were standard, and if the walls
were green it probably wasn't due to paint."
William Chadwick[75]

For the Sudeten Social Democrat families orbiting the city centre, their makeshift camps they now called home were rapidly deteriorating from their already semi-habitable state. Not only were the living conditions unfit for animals, let alone humans, this part of the Europe has some of the coldest winters in the continent, meaning the occupants were only just able to survive the conditions. For Warriner, such suffering under her nose was hard to bear, especially as she felt the guilt of returning each evening to her warm, comfy and safe hotel room. It was these sights which had driven her to the point of writing such a bitter letter to a newspaper a few months before. She did, however, use these traumatic sights to the advantage of her cause.

Each time well-wishers would present themselves at her offices wanting to help by donating a tiny sum of money, enough to buy a pint of milk, with the intention of heading home with a satisfactory feeling of contentment. As the mist of anger would descend on Warriner, she had taught herself to bottle it and would instead suggest they visit a camp before making any donations. Such was the suffering and squalor which confronted them, these people who witnessed it first-hand would then dig deep into their pockets to provide meaningful funds for relief. Warriner enlisted Winton among others to act as a tour guide for such trips, as she did not want any of these people to avoid seeing the camps in full.

One such visitor was a politician who arrived at the BCRC offices on 14th January called Sir Harold Hales, who had been the MP for Hanley until 1935. He met Winton on the plane to Prague, having arrived with the intention of selling motorcycles. Winton had gently explained that "business might not be good under current conditions" and that he could better use his time philanthropically.[76] After a few days, Hales took Winton's suggestion seriously and agreed to meet.

Hales owned and ran a large shipping company called Hales Brothers, founded the "Hales Trophy" for the fastest transatlantic crossing and was one of the first recorded humans to have crashed an airplane. His political career was even more colourful, with him adamantly campaigning for the use of car horns being made illegal in Britain and debating the decline of the herring industry in the House of Commons whilst gesturing with a dead herring in his left hand and his notes in his right. He had also been friends with the then recently deceased author

Arnold Bennett, whose protagonist in the novel The Card, was supposedly based on Hales.

On 14th January, another British Politician also visited the BCRC. Eleanor Rathbone MP was an independent British politician who had predicted the threat of Hitler since 1936 and subsequently campaigned against appeasement towards him. She was in the area to see for herself the impact of the Munich Agreement, which she had adamantly opposed in Parliament. She had also continually raised the question of the refugee crisis across Europe in Parliament. Nearing the age of 70, Rathbone was a formidable character with piercing eyes, grey hair tied up in a bun and had no interest whatsoever in fashion. As Winton explained "she never dressed, she just covered herself."[77]

Warriner saw the sincere wish of both these individuals, in particular Rathbone, to provide meaningful support. She knew this in part because she was an excellent judge of character, but also because Gilles had phoned ahead to tell her. They were both of considerable wealth and influence. Rathbone had conceived the idea for the Parliamentary Committee on Refugees, on which she was Honorary Secretary and Grenfell was Vice-Chairman. She had called in help from her wide network of influential figures, leading a deputation of the National Council for Civil Liberties on 19th October 1938 to the Foreign Secretary, Lord Halifax, for the protection of the Sudeten Germans. Among this group was civil rights campaigner Ronald Kidd and HG Wells, the renowned author of the aptly named "War of the Worlds.".

Winton was chosen to escort these two important guests, as he was arguably the most polished among the BCRC. He was under strict instructions from Gillies, through Warriner, that they should be given the best possible treatment while not being shielded from any unpleasant sights, sounds or smells which were now common in the camps. He was also instructed to watch over Rathbone carefully as she was notoriously forgetful and would often misplace her belongings wherever she went, evident in a recent trip she had made to Bucharest where she somehow "mislaid her coat and umbrella."[78]

The intended smooth running of the tour did not quite materialise. Winton managed to lose Hales after only a few minutes in the first camp, so continued the tour with Rathbone alone for the next few hours. They eventually found Hales sitting alone, head in hands, crying like a baby. Despite being a very typically British stiff-upper-lipped gentleman of the time who had witnessed his fair share of atrocities during his time with British Army in Turkey during World War I, the suffering in the camp was too much for him. Winton decided that they had seen their fair share, so suggested they withdraw. He quickly had to return to retrieve Rathbone's handbag, which had strayed from her grasp as they had been reunited with Hales, before retreating for a second time.

That evening, Winton wrote to his mother explaining the magnitude to the task which lay ahead of him. He was clear in his letter that if he was going to be successful in rescuing the children, he would need to avoid the existing communities who were also trying to help. There are countless examples from this time which show how, although there were so many well-meaning individuals who wanted to help, their bureaucracy, lack of organisation and desire to follow the rules, often made them more of a hindrance than a help. This opinion was doubtlessly formed in part from witnessing the political tensions which Warriner was now embroiled in.

CHAPTER 12

TIME IS RUNNING OUT

"It would be a race against time."
Doreen Warriner[79]

The 4th January 1939 was a significant day for the BCRC for two reasons. Both were extreme in their own right, one positive and the other negative.

The good news was the release of funds from the British support for Czechoslovakia worth £10 million, £4 million of which was a gift. In the terms, it allowed for up to 5,000 Sudeten refugees (£200 per family) to support them with their travel and settlement abroad. Although this had been announced by Chamberlain in October 1938, it had taken time to be put before Parliament and then for the funds to reach operations on the ground. For the rescue operation, this meant that they were no longer relying on the donations of organisations and individuals, which were now slowing down due in part to Warriner's letter to The Telegraph.

As soon as the money was pledged by the British Government, the Canadian authorities wasted no time in announcing that they were willing to take up to 1,200 families, stating by cable "we will take the people if the money is there."[80] At the time, the Canadian railways were so powerful they had more control and influence on immigration than the government. The railways had always relied on immigrants to fill their trains, usually coming from Germany or Scandinavia, but these numbers had slowed down due to the European conflicts. Canada was not haunted by Trade Unions in the same way many European countries were, especially Britain. Immigration always received heavy opposition from the unions in Britain on the grounds of possible job losses for their members. European countries were also struggling with unemployment rates, mostly as a consequence of the Great War.

This news meant that Warriner was able to resume transport with immediate effect. No longer was money an obstacle for her. For the BCRC in Prague, their job would be to get people to London – from there, it would be decided if they remain in Britain or go on further.

On the flip side, the bad news was the appearance of expulsion papers around Prague, ordering those who had opposed the Nazi regime to leave the country by 31st January or expect to be called for by Hitler. Warriner was sceptical of this, believing that it was simply a way for the Czech government to exert pressure on foreign governments to accept refugees. She pointed out that "when Hitler wanted people, he asked for them – and got them without fixing a date."[81] Nevertheless, it was at this point that even the most optimistic residents in Prague no longer questioned if their country would be occupied, but when it would be occupied.

More so than ever before, time was running out for the BCRC. There was a great step in the right direction for Warriner, when she received a call from Layton in London on 24th January saying that further transports for those in the camps had now been agreed, thanks to the British loan. The BCRC office in Prague had not been sitting idly for the past month. They had hundreds of men on standby to leave at a minute's notice. The next day, the first group of 20 Germans and Austrian men departed via KLM plane from the camps heading to Britain.

The men were too nervous to travel on boat through the Kiel Canal as it was suggested that the boats could be intercepted by the Nazis. As Warriner pointed out, this was an unlikely scenario, given the fact that Hitler could easily summon any of the refugees before they left and avoid a likely international incident – not that he was trying to avoid such incidents of course.

Nevertheless, this method of rescue quickly took priority over the trains, most likely as it was seen to be safer and quicker, with the fact that now money was not in such short supply. The downside was that these planes only had 20 seats, meaning the large rescue operations of the past were not possible. Documents are unclear, but we can assume that four further planes carrying adults left after this.

CHAPTER 13

THEN THERE WERE THREE

"We got a clear impression of the enormity of the task... and we saw only the fringe of it all... I felt that I had to do more about it."
Trevor Chadwick[82]

Over the next couple of days in early January 1939, the diary was no less busy for Warriner and Winton. It was in fact during these few days that the third main character of our story joins the team. Trevor Chadwick accompanied by a colleague, Geoff Phelps, arrived in Prague, having been sent there by Forres School in Swanage, which was now run by Chadwick's uncle. The school had sent the two of them in an attempt to bring a couple of refugee children back to Britain, to be looked after by the school for the duration.

On their arrival, they met Warriner, who quickly introduced them to Winton, given his evolving remit of looking after the children's side of the operation. The men chose two boys, Willi Weigl and Peter Walder to take back to Forres

School. They also took a girl, Gerda Mayer, who was to be cared for by Chadwick's mother. While they were in Prague, they toured many refugee camps, seeing for themselves the many lost and confused children without parents, as young as two years old. Unlike many others who visited, Chadwick realised that he was only seeing the outskirts of the real problem. For many, the ability to save three children, give them a home and a new family, would have been enough – but not for Chadwick. He immediately offered his full services to the BCRC.

On 21st January, Winton and Chadwick returned to Britain with the three children Chadwick had collected. Gilles had arranged for a lady named Mrs A. E. Guthrie and a Civil Servant called Creighton to act as interim leaders of the Children's Section of the BCRC whilst they were both in Britain.

There was no question that these two appointments were temporary, as both Winton and Chadwick were fully committed to driving the children's rescue. They agreed that Winton would remain in London to deal with the bureaucratic and administrative side of the operation, while Chadwick would be the man on the ground back in Prague. Quite in character for Chadwick, with no prior warning, took leave of absence from his Latin teaching duties and offered himself to the cause. Winton was a little less brash, agreeing to balance his job with his new extracurricular activity.

During their time together in London, Chadwick and Winton were busy visiting various charity organisations, including The Quakers and the Movement for the Care of Children from Germany, both of which were doing brilliant work to evacuate children from Germany and Austria, finding guarantors and foster families throughout Britain.

The two men were able to convince them to expand their remit to take children from Czechoslovakia, given that as refugees they would have likely come from Germany in the first place. The groups were strict that they would only be able to take a small number as their books were already overrun, emphasising that Winton and Chadwick would need another option for majority of the 760 children they had on their books. These charities were also putting into place the different puzzle pieces of bringing unaccompanied children into Britain, helping fill the gap in the BCRC's knowledge on the topic.

From his flat on Willow Road, Hampstead, Winton assembled a team which consisted of four individuals: Martin Blake, Barbara Willis, Winton and his mother, Barbara Winton. Willis was a young friend of Blake's who showed up unannounced one day to Winton's flat and offered to be his secretary.

While they set to work trying to arrange visas, transport and foster homes for nearly 800 children, Chadwick was high in the sky, heading back to Prague. Through their negotiations with the various London based children charities, he had agreed to find 20 children who would be adopted by foster families on these charities' knew. Chadwick had no problem in finding parents from their list to agree to their children flying to the safety of Britain.

He personally accompanied the group of children on the 20 seat airplane. Chadwick had a young baby on his lap all the way. As he recalls, "I took my first air transport rather proudly.

(The children) were all cheerfully sick, enticed by the little paper bags, except a baby of one who slept peacefully in my lap the whole time. The Customs Officers (in Britain) were a little puzzled and began to open some of the suitcases, which contained the kids' worldly treasures. But when I explained the position they were completely co-operative. Then there was the meeting with the guarantors – my baby was cooed over and hustled off, and the other nineteen were shyly summing up their new parents, faces alive with hope for the love they were obviously going to be given."[83]

Records of the time are unclear, but according to accounts by both Chadwick and Warriner, Chadwick and Winton flew multiple plane-loads of children back to Britain. Warriner recalls that "Winton began to get his children's transports going and flew off with plane loads of Jewish children."[84] What is strange about this is that none of these plane journeys are mentioned in stories of Winton nor in books written about him, including his excellent biography, written by his daughter. We know that several planes took children to Britain before the Nazis entered Czechoslovakia, including one which was recorded to have left on 10th March 1939, carrying the children who Warriner had rounded up in late 1938. She writes that it was through Winton's organisation and under the management of Chadwick. It is likely that this was, if not the last, one of the last planes to leave the country, as on 15th March all air transport was cancelled, as Hitler's men marched into Prague.

In any case, an assumption can be made that these children were fostered by families found by the pre-existing charities already evacuating children from Germany and Austria.

Despite having successful rescues to his name, an office and a team, Winton was acting on behalf of the BCRC with no authority to do so at all. This was not due to a lack of trying, as Warriner had already written to Margaret Layton, the honorary secretary of the BCRC in London, asking for Winton to be granted the position of Secretary of the Children's section of the BCRC. She wrote how Winton was "ideal for the job. He has enormous energy, businessmen methods, knows the situation perfectly here... all he needs now is authority to go ahead."[85] She went on to say how she had "been trying for three months to get these children away, Save the Children have disclaimed responsibility, so have InterAid and our own committee is overburdened with more urgent things."[86] By this time Winton had made approaches to the Home Office and even created his own headed paper as "Secretary, Children's Section for the BCRC."[87] It would not be until 24th May 1939, several months later, that Winton was officially given this role.

In February Winton got a rather negative letter from Layton, informing him that the children's movement from Germany and Austria, Kindertransport, would be unlikely to be of any assistance. She did not know that they had already flown several children out of Prague through this route. These were clearly elements of his work she was aware of, as she warned that the "Home Office is always antagonised by a multiplication of applications" for refugee status.[88] She therefore had knowledge of his letters to the government department.

It was true that when Winton turned to the Baldwin Fund, he was told that due to insufficient resources they were unable to assist. It is fair to say that both the Kindertransport and the broader BCRC under Layton's control were incredibly stretched at this time and were therefore reluctant to expand their remit further. As a theme which has appeared continually through this story, there were so many people in need of help, organisations had to make the difficult choice of those they were unable to help.

Without funding or support from other charities, the Children's Section of the BCRC was on its own. Winton therefore needed to find other options.

He did this in many ways, one of which was to publicly appeal to the British population's good will through the powers of Fleet Street. One letter he wrote to a national newspaper and was printed, "Dear Sir, Tales of violence and war, treaties made and broken, concentration camps and social ostracism have become so commonplace in the daily papers that the average person has completely lost his normal moral standard. A few years ago the publication of a story about a number of refugees without nationality or home who were starving in No Man's Land, not allowed admission but one country by being expelled by the other, would most certainly at the very least have made people stop and think. Now they are too inured to such tragedies to consider how they might be able to mitigate such suffering."[89]

Another report he issued to the press a few months earlier stated how "it may not be generally known that (by this time) only 25 children... have been brought out of Czechoslovakia" into Britain.[90] In this, he is referring to those he had seen leave on 12th January from the airport. He goes on to write how the condition for this was "if they were Jewish, that they should be baptised" into the Christian church, which was a condition which was seen later in the rescue operation.[91]

Winton had already formulated a plan for the Children's Section. He would scattergun requests around the country, through adverts in the press, contacting large organisations and utilising his many contacts. He needed to find people who were willing to adopt children for an undefined length of time.

Soon the British public responded to him, with individuals and families coming forward to offer their spare rooms. Winton quickly found that people had specific requirements when it came to who they were going to adopt. This surprised the BCRC's London team, as responses would come asking for just a boy or girl, and sometimes requesting an age or even specific looks.

To deal with this, they had photo cards printed with six children on each. Not only would this mean that foster parents would have their own choice, Winton knew that sending pictures of children, with some details about their background, would help them to gain sponsorship, as it is harder to say no when one has seen what one is saying no to. He would ask each foster parent to mark the child they wanted to sponsor with an "X". It is clear now why Matej Mináč named his book of the rescue "Nicholas Winton's Lottery of Life." He wrote "I thought how unjust life was and how senselessly cruel it can be... on some cards, two photographs were crossed out, on others three, on another only one, and there were many on which none of the photographs were crossed out. I knew very well that those children whose photographs were not crossed out had simply had bad luck.... they had not been selected, and so they perished."[92]

As photo cards would be returned to Winton's London address, his team would immediately cross them off their list and get a message to Prague. They then faced the task of accumulating all the necessary documentation for the Home Office, in order to gain the necessary visas. This in turn would be sent to Voršilská Street, where Warriner's team would then gain all the necessary approvals from the Czech side.

In Prague, Chadwick's remit was continuing to expand. Not only was he running the Children's Section with Winton, he was also providing essential help to the whole BCRC. For the children, each time he would receive notice from London that a child had been chosen for a new home across the sea, he would immediately contact the parents to inform them of the news. The parents would be told to have their children ready to leave at any minute, while also being instructed on how much, or how little in this case, they were able to travel with.

Between the three, Winton, Chadwick and Warriner, a smooth running and effective operation was taking shape. They had already evacuated several children by plane, although numbers are not known. They were now putting the pieces in place for transports which could take over 10 times the amount of children as the planes. They had their sights set on trains.

They had planned for almost all eventualities except one – what happens if Hitler arrives before the children can get out? In early March, no one knew if it was a matter of days, weeks or months. They knew it was only a matter of time.

***

Meanwhile, the adult section of the BCRC, the core at which it had been founded was also dealing with a race against time. So far 300 adults, nearly all male, had been swept away to Britain.

Warriner still had over 600 women and children she wanted to evacuate, a number which shocked the BCRC in London. She took the decision to fly back to Britain in the hope of speeding up the process. With pages of names in hand, she landed in London on 29th January. In a meeting with Gillies, Layton and the committee, she tried to put forward her reasons for using the loan money on the families of those they had already rescued. It was explained to her in polite terms that the money was to be used for people in immediate danger, which they felt these families were not. Warriner knew this was not the case, arguing passionately about the inevitability of Hitler's invasion and his disdain for all democratic Germans, whether they be male, female or children. He would arrest anyone he could. But the committee adamantly argued against this, leaving Warriner in despair. She wrote years later, "In Prague we lived on tenterhooks, but London were detached and calm... it was impossible to get through the cotton wool which prevented them from hearing."[93]

She left the meeting distraught, believing that there was no way of getting the families out. As the committee had pointed out, Winton and Chadwick were completely self-sufficient when it came to funding the children's evacuation – they were not asking for money from the British loan. They explained the parameters of the loan, and families were not part of it.

What Warriner did not know was that straight after the meeting, Gilles had whisked up the list of 600 names and taken it straight to Foreign Office, where it was miraculously approved without question. The committee would only find out months later.

Over the next three days, Warriner went from office to office in London. She was determined to streamline the process as best she could. One in particular which would save 100s of lives was in stamping passports. Up to this time, all documents were being sent by post, taking over three weeks to arrive in Prague. Warriner made a deal with the Home Office that they would start sending these by air, taking only a day. It meant that Warriner would be able to get visas approved in a couple of days, rather than several weeks.

On 2nd February, she flew back to Czechoslovakia reenergised. She had a new process arranged, funding and the visas agreed for 600 families. Back in Prague, as the sun began to melt the icy streets, Warriner rushed to Taub's office to tell him the news. This was what they had been waiting so many months for.

Working from 8 a.m. until the early hours of the following morning, Warriner, her three assistants Taub, Patz and Mollik were sorting the arrangements. Visas would arrive from London by the plane load, which would be assigned to passports, taken to the various consulates for stamps and finally reunited with their owners.

The largest group to leave in one load was on 15th February, described by Warriner as the climax of the rescue, with 500 individuals on board, 250 of whom went to Britain and the other 250 on to Sweden. That evening, at 11 p.m., a train stood full at Wilson Station – with family members standing on the platform waving. It is clear that although the refugees would have rather travelled by plane, it was a hopeless cause trying to get so many out of the country in groups of just 20. Here, in one group, 500 were leaving, five times more than all the air trips combined.

This took the total of rescued Sudeten refugees to 850, 250 in the first groups in 1938 and then the further 100 by plane and now 500 by train in 1939.

Although this is an astonishing feat, Warriner was the first to acknowledge the hundreds, even thousands more political refugees who needed saving. She also knew this number was just a fraction of the overall number of people who were in grave danger of Hitler's advance. Nevertheless, she wrote at the time that "February was wonderful." [94] However, for many reasons, she would not say the same for March.

CHAPTER 14

THE ADVANCE OF THE NAZIS

*"The army drove in like a Victory Parade, while the Czechs
looked on sullenly, sadly realising that their
few years of freedom were over."*
Robert Stopford[95]

In early March, a plump priest called Father Tiso was being
driven along the streets of Berlin. He had been collected by an
escort of soldiers from the airport and was being thrown around
in the back of the black staff car, which was being driven by a
youthful and impatient man. The priest was wearing his usual
attire: black shirt and trousers, white clerical collar and a thick
double breasted overcoat.

He was not on his way to carry out Holy Orders. Father
Jozef Gašpar Tiso was the Prime Minister of Slovakia, under the
ultimate control of the Czech government. After the Munich
Agreement, Tiso had taken advantage of the annexation of the
Sudetenland by attempting to declare Slovakia as a free state.
With this in mind, he was on his way to see the only man he felt

could make his vision a reality. He was due to meet with the leader of the Third Reich and ask for his assistance. Strategically for Hitler, Slovakia was important as it underpinned both Poland and Czechoslovakia, and was therefore only too happy to assist.

Thinking he now had the most powerful man in Europe on his side, Tiso returned from his secret meeting to Slovakia with optimism. Unfortunately for him, Czech Prime Minister, Rudolf Beran, had been tipped off about these treacherous talks.

Summoned to see Beran immediately after his return, Tiso was given one chance to terminate all conversations with Berlin. Flatly refusing to turn away from his vision of Slovakia gaining its independence, Beran had no choice by to dismiss Tiso on 10th March 1939.

This resulted in mass riots throughout Slovakia, orchestrate by Ludaks, the name given to members of Tiso's loyal Slovak People's Party. This is important for our story as the Czech troops protecting Prague were sent over the border to implement martial law thus leaving the city exposed.

***

In Prague, it was reported to Warriner that Hitler was closing in and that concentration camps would be set up for any remaining refugees in and around Prague. The living conditions for the Sudeten Germans under the BCRC's control was less than comfortable, but at least they were in some way safe.

Although Warriner was under no illusion that the invasion of Czechoslovakia was not a matter of if, but when, she did not think it was that imminent. In fact, she was convinced that Hitler would want to take Slovakia first, which would take some time, leaving her enough of a window to get the remaining refugees out of the country. She was unreliably informed that Slovakia would not fall without a fight – such was the general opinion around Europe.

However, news began to filter through to the BCRC from some of their underground sources that there was unrest in Slovakia, and that the Prime Minister was due to be replaced. Information was unclear, but there were rumours that the Slovakians would make a deal with Hitler and therefore not face any military aggression. This scenario would mean Czechoslovakia would be surrounded from all sides, except to the north with Poland, by the Nazis.

On Saturday 11th March, the BCRC in London received a telegram from a panicked Warriner, "Situation very uncertain. Committee should prepare emergency plan."[96] Back in Britain, the scenario in Europe was less apparent, and the committee did not treat this telegram with the urgency which Warriner had intended. As Warriner had originally predicted, Slovakia provided valuable time for Czechoslovakia. Even by the 13th March, when the London team congregated for their weekly meeting, they were unable to decide what should be done with the remaining Sudeten Democrats still in the camps and most importantly, whether they were actually in serious enough danger to warrant their departure.

Although this attitude was unacceptable to Warriner and provided her with high levels of stress and frustration, she also fell victim to complacency.

In fact, on Sunday 12th March, the people of Prague began to relax a little as the prospect of the Nazi advance seemed to grind to a crawl. Warriner could not understand why as at the back of her mind she still believed the Czech's days were numbered. What had actually happened was typical of the Nazis. They would call off the propaganda mission ahead of the military invasion. This was metaphorically the calm before the storm.

Back in Slovakia on this day, Tiso was replaced as Prime Minister, the appointee being by the name of Sidor, who immediately refused the demands of Hitler. He was appointed to keep the country part of the Czech empire. By this time it was too late as momentum drummed up by Tiso was too strong. Four days later Slovakia was declared independent and the Nazi war machine rolled into the country. Slovakia became its own republic, gaining Protectorate status with Germany.

For Warriner the timing was bad, but for Winton and Chadwick it was a disaster for their Children's Section. It was by awful coincidence that that day, 12th March, was earmarked for their first ever train evacuation of unaccompanied children. The events of the previous week had meant Chadwick was unsure about sending the children away, but as the news began to die out, he felt a sense of optimism. Indeed he told Winton that the train would be leaving on the evening of 12th March and he should therefore expect the arrival the next day in Liverpool Street Station.

The takeover of Slovakia became too much for the BCRC, who quickly sent a telegram saying, "Transport postponed. Probably Tuesday." They rightly wanted to verify reports before sending children through Europe alone. The next day, Chadwick was satisfied and decided to push ahead with what would be the first of many Kindertransports from Prague.

On 14th March, standing on the smoky and damp platform of Liverpool Street Station was Nicholas Winton and his mother. They watched with anticipation as the huge, green menacing steam train pulled into the station on its final stop of its journey. From one of the carriages emerged 20 tired children, all wrapped warmly in their coats and scarves. All 20 of them had a luggage label hanging around their neck.

Winton had known that the train was on its way, as the day before he had received a telegram signed by Warriner and Chadwick, simply saying "congratulations". [97] This was the smallest trainload of children to leave Prague, but was no doubt deliberately small so as to test the reliability of this method of transport. It is also the same number of children who had travelled over by plane. For everyone concerned, this was a huge success and the moment which Winton and Chadwick realised that their list of 760 children they had complied months before, might actually be a realistic target. This was a major success, but in the wider scheme of the rescue, there was no time for Warriner and her team to celebrate.

***

It was Monday 13th March 1939, early morning and bitterly cold. The rumour mill was turning non-stop, with stories of the Nazis arriving any minute rattling around everyone's households, even though the newspapers and wirelesses had ceased reporting it. No one really knew the situation in Slovakia, only that there was a lot of unrest in the streets. Warriner was receiving mixed messages, on the one hand Eric Crowe, one of Legation secretaries was saying that these rumours were fabricated and that no such threat existed. On the other hand, Harold Gibson, the passport worker, was telling her that these rumours were under exaggerated and that the situation was worse and more threatening that she was hearing. She decided to get the advice of Robert Stopford, the main liaison between the Czech government and the refugees.

She met him for lunch and they discussed the urgency needed. He reassured her that they still had time before the Germans would arrive – although Warriner was not given any idea of how long. After their meal and while they were sipping their filter coffee, he dropped a bombshell saying that "it may be impossible to get (the people on Warriner's lists) away," as he was concerned with them being able to cross the Polish border.[98] His worry stemmed from the fact that if the Polish government found out about Slovakia, they would soon shut off their borders completely in anticipation of the takeover of their neighbour, Czechoslovakia. He was not giving up and told her he would go back to the legation and see what could be done, if anything. Warriner agreed that she would meet him there at 4 p.m. to hear the results of his investigations.

What was becoming ever apparent was that they simply did not have the time to get each visa assigned one by one, which had been happening up to this point. Despite the negotiations which Warriner had had with the British Foreign Office on her last visit, each visa document still needed approving separately. Luckily, Stopford was of the same mind and issued a memo to the British Foreign Office saying that Warriner's lists should be treated as a priority and that the Czech government was doing so as well.

The issue they still faced was that even if they got a "group visa" from London, it did not seem likely that the Polish government would accept this, as they would only issue a travel visa through Poland once they had physically seen the British visa in the refugee's passport, which in this case would not be possible. This was an ongoing theme for the rescue operation, when one government would agree to one thing and the other government would refuse it. Warriner, the master of negotiation and diplomacy at this point, went straight to the Polish Consulate to see what could be done, and sure enough she was able to agree a compromise. They said they would give their stamp of approval only once they could physically see the British had approved the list.

Warriner was immediately on the phone to Gillies, explaining the situation to him and asking for him to support the departure of the refugees, even if the committee would not. She needed a decisive answer and, in his true form, Gillies gave her one.

"Put all the women and children on a train at once," he instructed.[99]

This was exactly the answer which Warriner wanted – it was now on Gillies to organise everything on the London side of the operation, i.e. getting the visas approved *en masse*, as Stopford had suggested. Excitedly Warriner suggested a departure date of Wednesday 15th March, just two days from then, which she knew would be a challenge. Gillies was having none of it, as he knew they had no time to spare, barking down the phone, "No, tomorrow!"[100]

It was now 10.30 p.m. on Monday evening and Warriner had under 24 hours to arrange the departure of 700 women and children, on a train due to leave at 11 p.m. the following day. At this exact moment, Hitler was having a face-to-face meeting with the newly unemployed Tiso, whom he had summoned to Berlin and ordered him to return to Slovakia and declare its independence, which he did.

At 6.30 a.m. on Tuesday 14th March, just over 16 hours before the departure from Wilson Station was scheduled, Warriner and Hilde Patz were desperately sending out telegrams to the various refugee camps. Some of these temporary homes were over 10 hours from Prague by train, meaning they would have a very tight window to achieve, what seemed likely to be their last chance of escape. Nevertheless, this did not prey on either Patz or Warriner's minds, as they had more pressing issues at hand. Although Gillies had given them the green light to get the 700 women and children out, they still did not have any visas nor any word as to whether the British Foreign Office would agree to stamp the list as a whole. The timing of this would have a knock on effect with the Polish consulate, who were willing to give their approval, but would only do so while they were open, meaning that if the word from London came after the Polish consulate was closed, the train would need to be delayed until the following day, which could be too late.

The day was painstaking for Warriner and her team, a feeling like none other and one she would never forget. Back and forward she would drive between the British Legation and her office, hoping each time for some news, instructions or ideally the stamped list. But throughout the morning and then into the afternoon, her trips were always in vain. On each of her return visits to her headquarters, the corridors, rooms and even her own office were filling up with refugee women and children, exhausted after travelling all day, but in high spirits at the prospect of leaving. They were having their names added to a definitive list, and being sent to Wilson Station. By 6 p.m., there were no less than 500 women and children at the train station, with a further 200 supposedly en route. It is hard to imagine what the ideal scenario for Warriner and her team was at this point. Do they hope the approval from London arrives in time and that the train departs that evening as planned, leaving 200 women and children stranded, or that train is delayed, but gives the 200 absentees enough time to board?

This question was irrelevant by 7 p.m., as Warriner got the nod from London. Gillies had managed to arrange for the list presented by Warriner to be stamped. She rushed to the British Legation where the Passport Officer had permission to stamp her list of 500. In the sub-zero temperatures, she then sped to the Polish Consulate, where she had managed earlier that day to persuade the Vice-Consul, a small and kind gentleman, to remain in the office late. Luckily he was a man of his word and was waiting for her to arrive, and when she did, he provided his collective stamp of approval for all 500 on this list, as he could see the British had done the same.

With little time to spare, as she was leaving the consulate she was pounced on by the Čedok currier, who used his strength to remove the list and all 500 passports from Warriner. It is possible that he was hoping to send the party by boat on the Gdynia-American line, which they had tried a few months prior. Warriner screamed and shouted as this assault unfolded, as she was desperate not the let the stamped documents and passports out of her safekeeping. Given the trouble they had previously had with Čedok and Polish representatives in the past, it is understandable why she got so upset by this. Luckily two officials she knew well from the Consulate heard the commotion as they were leaving and came to her rescue. Given their rank, they were able to tell the courier in no uncertain terms to leave what he had taken and be on his way, which he did.

Shaken, but still focused, Warriner was on her way to the train station when she realised that there was something she had completely overlooked. In all the confusion and rushing around, she had forgotten about the money from the News Chronicle fund, which was in the bank. It was assumed that this would be the safest place to store £5,000, however they knew that Hitler would clean out all the money he could get his hands on, without exception. Warriner made a detour to the bank, where she made a withdrawal of the whole fund, meaning she had wads of cash and hundreds of passports and visas with her. Only later would she realise the amount of pressure she was under at this point.

At this time, Jaksch was desperately clearing out his office on Fochova Street, making sure everything was destroyed for "no-one should be put at risk by a letter or note left behind."[101] He was offered a place on the train, but refused to leave city.

By 9 p.m. Warriner was at Wilson Station, arranging the logistics and handing out the passports to all those waiting. Ingman was the designated courier to accompany the group. The train was loaded and as planned, at 11 p.m. the wheels started moving with 500 women and children on board. 200 were still absent and Warriner had no explanation for this, leaving her worried and bemused. At this point, it seems that the 500 were out of danger. But this was not the case.

It was 2 a.m. on Wednesday 15th March, only three hours after the train had left and one hour after Warriner's head had finally hit the pillow, when the phone rang with Margaret Layton on the other end. She suggested to Warriner that her job was now complete and that she should return to Britain – Prague was now too dangerous for her and any further efforts were pointless. Warriner had an insatiable ambition to save everyone without exception and unsurprisingly now we have got to know her, she did not agree, not least because she did not know the fate of the train, but also because there were still people in danger who had not been able to escape. What had happened to the 200 missing women and children? She thought that over the next three days, she would have time to get the final few refugees from the country.

It was at 4 a.m. on Wednesday 15th March that the train which Warriner had seen off the night before reached Ostrava, where it was stopped by the Nazis, who had taken the area moments before. Luckily, they were still getting organised and were not too attentive or aware of who should be stopped and who should be allowed through. Ingman was quick witted about the situation, aware of the danger they were now in, and ordered all the blinds to be shut on the train as it was grinding to a halt by command of a Nazi officer. When the train came to a standstill and the Germans approached, Ingram confronted them in a jovial manner, jesting "you'll never guess what I've got here: A load of dirty Jews."[102] This was met by roars of laughter from the Germany troops, who exchanged some derogatory remarks about Judaism, before shaking hands with Ingman and waving the train on its way. Had it been discovered that the train actually contained hundreds of wanted women and children, the results would have been disastrous for all on board and would have left Ingman with some impossible explaining to do. Later that morning, Warriner received a telegram from Ingman saying "all well", and so another 500 were saved with only a few hours to spare. Getting political refugees out by train was likely to no longer be an option, as the route they were taking would mean now being stopped by the Nazis, who would likely be more rigorous for any further transports. They were still willing to let Jews out of the country, as Hitler's original plan was for them to leave, before introducing his notorious "Final Solution" two years later.

At 6 a.m., Warriner was only starting to drift back to sleep, with her mind racing around her head, thinking up different scenarios and methods to overcome them. Just as her mind started to go blank, the telephone rang again. It was Reed, a volunteer from her office, informing her that the Nazis had now crossed the frontier and were making their way to Prague. They had been given no resistance and there was nothing which would slow them down. He told her that it was now a matter of hours before the jack boots would be sounding down the streets of the capital.

Reed rushed over to pick Warriner up and they drove franticly to the KLM headquarters, where the air agent lived. It was only just turning 7 a.m. and their banging on his door woke him. Invasion or no invasion, he was less than happy to be dragged from his bed. He was in quite a daze and had not heard the news that the Nazis were apparently only hours away. He told them that it was too dangerous for any planes to depart, as they had been given instructions that all such transport should be postponed until further notice. As Warriner noted in her diary that evening, "So they were trapped."[103] With the planes no longer being an option, they fell back onto the idea of trains, knowing only too well that they would need to travel through Nazi controlled borders, smuggling the people who the Gestapo would be searching for.

By 8 a.m., Warriner was entering her office, for what would be the final day. Similar to the day before, the halls were lined with refugees, desperate to escape in any way possible, many of who were meant to be on the train the night before. Warriner still did not know if the 500 were safe, as far as she was concerned, those now in her headquarters might have been the lucky ones. The refugees entered Warriner's office family by family. Those who had turned up, but were not on the original list of 700 were given cash and told to try and get to the border at Katowice, where she knew the British Consulate would be able to support them. Those on the list of 700, technically already had a visa to travel through Poland and on to Britain as the others were doing by train. Warriner therefore gave them money, a signed visiting card and a note to the Consul saying they were permitted to travel. Despite the financial and official support, these families were on their own and needed to try and get out in any way they could. Warriner told them that she was trying to organise transport, now likely to be another train, and that it was up to them whether they wanted to wait or go on by themselves. It is unknown how many made the journey on their own, although there are several records of people making their way to Poland and crossing the border illegally.

It was later that morning when Warriner received the news she had been waiting for. A telegram arrived from Ingman simply saying "all well."[104] The 500 were safely through the Nazi occupied Slovakia and were now in the safety of Poland, heading for the coast, where a boat waited to take them to Britain.

It is safe to say that Warriner enjoyed this feeling of success for about one second, before her mind raced back to the task in hand – those who were now trapped in Prague. She realised that remaining in her office was pointless, as there was nothing she could really achieve there, but advise each refugee individually. She needed a plan which would help them en mass. It was also a very well-known destination for any political refugees to seek assistance, meaning that the Nazis would prioritise it as a place to shut down.

As with many of Warriner's predictions, she was completely right and later that evening, the door to the building was kicked in and soldiers burst in to search it. The office had been their headquarters for several months now and was therefore very 'lived in' with documents scattering all possible working areas meaning it was difficult to know what to collect, what to leave and what to destroy. It was in some confusion that they collected all the passports and as many documents they felt would be needed, telling the refugees there to leave as soon as possible. Tessa Rowntree recalled an evening of "tearing up passports and papers and flushing them down the lavatory."[105] It was in this confusion that they forgot to destroy some of what was left and even left some passports, which each thought one of the others was taking responsibility for. They went back to Warriner's hotel, The Alcron, where they set up a temporary office.

By midday, the Nazis had arrived. The city which so many people fled to for safety was now Hitler's latest conquest. The country that represented the freedom from the German oppression after the previous World War, was no longer free or safe.

The Alcron Hotel, being one of the nicer hotels in Prague, was now filled with the most senior Nazi officers, all trying to earmark this destination as their new home away from home. For Warriner, only a few hours prior, she had been collected from an empty lobby, of a fairly quiet building, in the attempt to help wanted individuals evade the Nazis. On that very day and just a few hours later, she was entering the same building which was now the nerve centre of the people she had been so desperately opposing.

As Warriner and Dougan walked past reception, one of the staff called after them, telling Warriner she had a call from London waiting for her, which she took from the lobby phone.

It was Miss Rathbone, asking her to pass over any names she still needed visas for, as Rathbone said she was able to get any approved that day. It is quite the scene to imagine: an eccentric British politician giving her orders from her Westminster office to Warriner, who was completely surrounded by The German General Staff, making a racket as they tried to check into the hotel of a country they had invaded that morning.

Nevertheless, Rathbone's call was reassuring for Warriner, so she set off, leaving Dougan urgently shedding and burning all the lists, papers and correspondents in Warriner's room.

Warriner was heading for the British Legation again, picking up Patz and Mollik, where she found Jaksch, Taub, his wife and son and a few others. They had rushed there in order to seek refuge from the Nazis. This group was probably the most in danger from the start, but they had flatly refused to leave until all their party members were out, the captain being the last to leave the sinking ship. The Minister of the Legation was in a state of despair and terror, telling the group that if they were asked for by the Nazis, he would not apply diplomatic rights and hand them over without protest.

Jaksch was also frantic that, despite his activity the night before, he had left some papers in his office which he knew if they fell into the hands of the Germans, they would be very useful to them. Patz, who was as usual thinking straight, also wanted to return to Warriner's office to make sure there were no papers they had left behind. The two ladies were back on the road, driving across the city to get to their offices before the enemy could. By this time, the snow was becoming heavier than it had all day, meaning the roads were slow and treacherous, while also being packed with German tanks, military personnel carriers and armoured lorries, whose only opposition to entering the city was the weather.

It was when they reached their offices, they were able to spend the next few hours destroying as much of what was left as they could as well as everything in Jaksch's office. As they were about to leave, in a taxi now weighed down with suitcases of papers and files, Patz remembered a hiding place of passports of those 200 women and children who had not arrived the night before for the train. As we have seen, the BCRC would keep their passports in order to get visas for them to travel. Warriner ran back into the office to retrieve this, but as she approached the door, she heard two men conversing in German on the other side. From what she heard, which we do not know for sure, she recognised them as German police, so fled back to the taxi. Their mission was a success to the extent that they destroyed all they needed to, but they were leaving the passports of so many women and children wanted by the Nazis, meaning these people were now completely stranded. These passports would later be seized by the police and eventually handed over to the Gestapo.

Travelling back after only a few hours showed the speed and efficiency of the Nazis – the whole of Prague was being transformed with huge guns and giant swastikas hanging from all significant buildings. The snow was now heavier than it had been all day, making the journey even more treacherous. Warriner insisted on making a stop on the way back to one of the BCRC's helpers she had not heard from all day, Frau Schmoka, only to find her house completely wrecked. From the outside, all seemed normal, but as they approached the front door, they saw broken glass. Peering inside, the house was unrecognisable, as if a bomb at hit it. Schmoka had been arrested because of her anti-Nazi links and was now on her way to the notorious Pankrác Prison.

When back at the Legation, Warriner was voicing her concern about the others trying to escape while the streets were so busy. Surely, she thought, there is too much activity and too much intensity for Jaksch and Taub to escape unnoticed. But, as most of those in the room had seen Hitler's forces take over the Sudetenland, they knew that this was probably the safest time, as the soldiers were too busy installing themselves to worry about some refugees. The time to worry, they told Warriner, was when the dreaded Gestapo arrived. Although she was hesitant for their safety, given how quickly Schmoka had been taken, Warriner knew it was a race against time between Jaksch and Taub, as well as Patz who was well known by now and Mollik, whose two brothers were both Nazis. With Jaksch and Taub still bravely refusing to leave, Warriner accompanied Patz and Mollik to the Čedok office where they would collect their tickets to Poland, enabling them to escape that evening. Once there, she left both women to get together the necessary documents and they parted ways. Warriner commented in her diary that she was not too worried about them as she had known both for several months and knew them to be highly capable and resourceful.

It was now the middle of the night. The streets of Prague were deserted; all the vehicles and soldiers had quietened down. The city had gone through a transformation that day. Warriner was told it would be best for her to stay in the British Legation, as it was so late and too dangerous for her to make her own way back to her hotel. She was grateful to accept the invitation to stay in one of the Legation rooms. On the top floor, from her room window she could see the Castle, lit up brightly, showing all the swastikas hanging down. Inside slept the most dangerous man in the world – Adolf Hitler. He had come to the city that night in order to take part in the victory parade the next morning. Rumour has it that he saw the ghost of Tomáš Masaryk, the founder and first President of Czechoslovakia. The ghostly sighting apparently had such an effect on the Führer that he was unable to sleep for most of the night.

Thursday 16th March was no less busy for Warriner. Clearly a person who can operate on next to no sleep, she was awoken by two frightened refugee women. They had gone to her office that morning, but had walked into scene from a police drama novel, with officials in Nazi uniforms, policemen and men in suits swanning around. Warriner went with these women, who told her of many women and children, over 30 families, at the train station. These were many of those who had not managed to get back in time for the train which left a few nights prior, many of whom no longer had passports, something they were not yet aware of. Warriner fed them all in the station restaurant as none had eaten or slept all night, while Dougan tried to find some accommodation for these families which was a difficult task as all the central hotels were being used by the German soldiers. However, they found some rooms in a village on the outskirts of the city, where the innkeeper was willing to house the refugees for a week's payment in advance. As the day before has shown, nothing is that straightforward. As it was turning late morning, Hitler was parading through the streets of Prague, which meant that the city was in gridlock, with Wenceslas Square completely shut.

They therefore needed to go all the way around the city where they would be met by a bus to take them to the hotel. Scared of attracting unnecessary attention to themselves by walking in large groups, they tried to walk separately – not an easy task with so many children. Eventually, after a couple of stops for food and coffee, a fainting woman and several crying children, Warriner gave in when she saw a taxi rank, paying for them all to be driven to the bus and then on to their hotel. The news for Warriner once they finally arrived was accompanied with tales of even more women and children at the train station. So back and forward they went all morning, finding hotels where they could, most of which were grubby and dirty, but completely luxurious for the refugee women and children, who had been living in squalid camps for the past six months.

Over the coming days, Warriner and her team would make many of these trips, having a total of 240 women and children living in six hotels in and around the city. As the days went on, their situation got more and more dangerous. These women no longer had passports, which caused quite the challenge, one which was only just scratching the surface, as the Nazis introduced compulsory exit permits for everyone leaving the country. This meant that a visa for Britain, a travel visa through Poland, an entry permit for Poland, Passport, and an exit permit from Czechoslovakia were all required for each person. This new measure just shows how lucky the group of 500 had been to leave the night before the invasion.

As was usual for the Nazis by this point of taking over a country, the Gestapo arrived. As part of the SS and led by the Chief of German Police Heinrich Himmler, the Gestapo was the 32,000 strong German Secret Police. Sent to lead Gestapo operations in Prague was Kriminalrat Karl Bömelburg, a 54-year-old "elderly, smiling gentleman, far from sinister," as Chadwick later reflected. [106] Bömelburg arrived in Czechoslovakia following an assignment in Paris to investigate the assassination of German diplomat, Ernst vom Rath in 1938. The killing, carried out by Polish-German Jew Herschel Grynszpan was a very high profile case to be involved in, especially as Kristallnacht was launched hours after the attack. Bömelburg was chosen for this assignment partly down to merit, but more so because he lived as a child in France for five years and spoke the language well. He arrived in Prague after being expelled from Paris, accused of helping far-right extremists and Nazi sympathisers.

Stopford and Chadwick wasted no time in introducing themselves to Kriminalrat Bömelburg, with whom they "continued to negotiate with (for the) issue of exit permits."[107] The relationship they built up with him was essential to their continued successful transports. Bömelburg became known as "the criminal rat" to Warriner and her team, due to his unfortunate title, signifying he had been in his rank for under three years. Chadwick wrote in a letter years later "I remember my deep delight in the word Krininalrat."[108] Stopford's ability to build a close tie with the Gestapo leaders was impressive, but given his status within the British Legation, it is no surprise. But for Chadwick, it is a true testament to his character that he was able to gain the trust and respect from the Germans. He recalled "they gave me an unpleasant time at first and I remember putting on the screaming table-thumping act – always reliable with those louts – and demanding an interview with the Kriminalrat... he made things easier for me."[109] His courage and bravery in being so direct with the Gestapo, a feared and deadly group, should not be underestimated.

Despite the arrival of the Gestapo, Warriner and her team were busy working on getting these women and children out of the country. They were able to get exit visas for those whose passports had not been lost, the only tricky part was that these needed to be obtained from the Gestapo directly, a task which Stopford and Chadwick took on with a huge amount of courage. This extra measure meant that Warriner was back where she had started with the process of gaining visas as each one needed approval on an individual basis. Nevertheless, slowly, her hotels began to empty over the next few weeks, whilst those left behind were becoming more and more nervous, voicing their concerns quite abruptly to those trying to help them.

Warriner tried to reassure them that they would be able to get the passports back. In fact, she was being genuine, as she had tried to bribe a senior member of the police to recover them. Sadly, although it seems the police officer did try, they were already with the Gestapo. As each day passed, Warriner would tell the women that she was certain they would have their passport the next day. After several weeks of these promises, the women were rapidly losing any hope of survival. Those who were able to leave either did so illegally through whatever underground organising was willing to help them and for those who were leaving legitimately, usually the women and children, the Gestapo was not being particularly stringent with their checks.

CHAPTER 15

THE GREAT ESCAPE

"Jaksch, on whom all the enmity of the Sudeten Nazi was concentrated...knew the (Nazis) would never let him go."
Doreen Warriner[110]

Wenzel Jaksch was now one of the most wanted men in Czechoslovakia. According to the Daily Herald, a price was placed on his head by the Germans, ordering the Gestapo to "get him dead or alive."[111] It would only be a matter of time before wanted posters with his face on them would appear throughout the streets of Prague. His whereabouts was a mystery to most, but not all.

Within the confines of the British Legation now lived several people, including Jaksch and Taub. They had spent several days hiding under the diplomatic cover of the British.

The British Legation was a large five-storey white building like so many of its neighbours, with a courtyard in the middle. As the crow flies, it is less than a five minute walk to the Castle, where the Fuhrer himself was staying. This convenient positioning for the British Legation staff in the centre of the city was less than ideal for a man on the run. When leaving the courtyard of the complex through the big black gates built into the wall at the front, one enters a narrow cobbled path which, framed by two high buildings, heads 20 yards before turning onto Thunovská Street. Where this cobbled path meets the street today stands a magnificent brass bust of Sir Winston Churchill, defiant looking with his hands gripping the lapels of his jacket. In March 1939, in his place were two undercover Gestapo Officers, leaning against the stone wall smoking an endless supply of cigarettes looking incredibly suspicious and not in any way subtle.

The Germans had correctly suspected that the disappearance of Jaksch was somehow related to the British. We know this because they tried to persuade Stopford that if he "surrender (Jaksch) to them they would intern him in a place of his own choice."[112] This was something neither Stopford nor Jaksch ever entertained as being true. According to Warriner, Jaksch had already "decided to escape, because he knew that they would never let him go."[113] Taub and the other Sudeten Democrats who had taken refuge with Jaksch in the British Legation were not high enough on the Nazi wanted list to warrant the same concern.

Describing himself as "the uninvited guest" of the Legation, Jaksch lived for a week in a makeshift bedroom, sleeping "on the red plush bench of the ballroom."[114] It was during this time that his illegal escape was being planned. Such an escape would not be straightforward. There was only one way in and out of the Legation, down the cobbled path, which was now under surveillance night and day. The trains out of Prague were being searched endlessly. The borders were now guarded by the Nazis, who were on high alert for the distinctive looking Jaksch. It has never been revealed whether any British officials helped Jaksch to escape, outside of them allowing him to seek refuge within the Legation. Scholar Dr Martin D. Brown believed he tried to escape "with Stopford's and the Foreign Office's connivance, if not their explicit support."[115]

Early on the morning of Tuesday 21st March, the spring weather was starting to appear, signalling an end to the bitter winter. A middle aged man called Kminek was making his way to work, dressed in his usual workman overalls of blue dungarees, a buttoned up grey shirt, boots and a large trench coat to keep out the cold. He wore a waxed flat cap, pulled low over his eyes. Kminek, a Czech metal worker, was weighed down by a heavy bag of tools slung over one shoulder and some six foot copper pipes balancing on the other.

The two poorly disguised Gestapo officers watching the cobbled path leading to the entrance of the British Legation took little notice of this man on this way to work, as he knocked on the towering black gates of the complex and was swiftly allowed in. They paid him even less attention when he exited from the courtyard a few hours later after his mornings toils and walked back down the cobbled path onto Thunovská Street and disappeared into the crowds of the city. In fact, such little attention was given by the German soldiers that they did not notice that it was a completely different person beneath the overalls. It was in fact Prague's most wanted man: Jaksch.

Warriner wrote later that "he looked like a workman, because he had been one," meaning it was an easy disguise for him to escape in.[116] He made his way quickly to Kminek's apartment, where he was met by his escape party. Consisting of an older Sudeten German called Sacher and two women, one of whom was Czech and other German, they spent the remainder of Tuesday 21st March preparing for their up-and-coming adventure. Kminek joined them later that night, having been able to slip out of the Legation without causing suspicion that evening. They had decided he should wait in the Legation until night, in case the Gestapo were counting people in and out. Kminek was the man who spearheaded the escape of his leader, as Warriner noted Kminek did so "throwing up his job and leaving his flat," which he would not return to during the occupation.[117]

Meticulous planning had been carried out by Jaksch's four accomplices for the previous week. The most difficult task they faced was obtaining false passports and travel permits, which would allow them to leave the country. It is not known exactly where they were able to get such paraphernalia from, but most of the characters in this story were involved in some form of illegal forgeries, albeit in a minor form. It was such that Stopford and Chadwick were often confronted on the topic by the Gestapo authorities. Stopford had discovered that Gestapo staff had "for a consideration been forging passports" themselves.[118] In any case, they were able to get hold of five forgeries in order to escape the country.

Because scrutiny was so high at Wilson Station, all five escapees were likely to be searched on multiple occasions before the train would leave. It was common by now for trains to be stopped from departing, everyone forced off and then searched again. This ritual would sometimes be repeated five times before the train would eventually depart.

It would therefore be impossible for anyone of the six travellers to carry their real identity cards with them. However, it was equally important that Jaksch had his real documentation to get into Britain, who would understandably not allow a German man to enter the country with fake documents. What they needed was someone who was willing to carry these documents across the border, into Poland and meet them in a pre-agreed location. There was only one person they knew they could trust and who would be willing to undertake such a personal risk – Warriner. She was unwavering with her willingness to carry out this task, which if caught, would certainly result in her imprisonment.

On Wednesday 22nd March, the escape party of five headed to Wilson Station, to catch a train east in the direction of Moravia.

Disguised as well-to-do winter sport enthusiasts, the two women wore bright knitted jumpers and the three men dressed in smart all-in-one ski outfits. The men carried sets of Flexible Flyer styled vintage skis over their shoulders and large backpacks full of supplies.

At Wilson Station, the midday sun sored through the front of the stained glass semi-circular window towering over the front entrance, lighting up the German soldiers on patrol.

The group of supposedly upper-class skiers were given surprisingly little hassle by the waiting soldiers and were allowed into their compartment. Jaksch noted that "there were six booked men with knapsacks" standing on the platform when they had arrived.[119] It became clear to the escape party that these men were from either the dreaded SS or Gestapo. To their dismay the six men were "steered straight to (their) car and filled the compartment next door.[120]

The ritual of the train being stopped and searched was skipped on this occasion, most likely because even ordinary German soldiers were afraid of the Gestapo, daring not to delay their journey.

Kminek, Sacher, Jaksch and the two women were relieved when the train drew out of the station, but also terrified that they were only separated from Gestapo officers by a thin wooden partition of the carriage.

For an unknown reason, the officers began to get suspicious of the five people in the next-door compartment. Was it the fact they were acting suspiciously, sitting completely still and had not muttering a word? Or was it because he knew they were given an easy exit from Wilson Station? Maybe the officers were bored and this was a way to pass the time? In any case, their leader walked through the corridor and entered the escape party's cabin. He began asking questions to the two women and three men about their business, where they were going and what their reason for their journey was.

Kminek immediately took the lead, explaining how they intended to ski near the border, as the snow was fresh and nearly completely untouched. This pricked the interest of the Gestapo officer, who was himself a keen skier and told the skiing group that he intended to try the same slopes for himself.

Soon, the officer had invited his subordinates from next door into Kminek's cabin and the 11 men and women began sharing stories, mostly about winter sports, with each other. Jaksch recalled that "from our backpacks we picked oranges, ham sandwiches and schnapps," the latter they shared with their new Nazi travel companions.[121]

Soon Kminek had a large map unfolded on the floor of the compartment, using his index finger to show the best slopes for the Gestapo men to try when they were off duty. Little did they know, Kminek was guiding them on the exact route he intended to take Prague's most wanted man, who was sitting in that very compartment. Jaksch went unnoticed, reporting afterwards that they "took him for a winter sports enthusiast," and paid him little attention in comparison to Kminek, whom had charmed them.[122] By this point, all 11 were laughing merrily, sharing drinks with each other and scribbling down map references for their favourite winter hobby. After some hours of this, the train drew into the Nazi group's stop, where they all shook hands with Kminek and his companions, before leaving the train.

A sense of relief descended on the five, albeit they felt a little groggy-eyed after hours of sipping an endless supply of vodka. Jaksch recalled years later that in response to each of the Nazis jokes during their journey, he would force himself to laugh which "sometimes came a little roughly from the throat."[123]

The escape party changed onto a small regional stopping train, heading for the Moravia-Slovak border. At its final station, they were the last people on the train, left standing in the mysterious dark of that Wednesday night. Being too late to travel any further that day, they tried to find shelter in a tourist hut near the train station. As the five approached, they saw men in black leather jackets and matching forage caps, with black tassels hanging off. This was unmistakably the uniform of the Hlinka Guard, a Slovakian Nazi-sympathising militia.

Luckily they were able to avoid this hut, as the Hlinka Guard were notoriously ruthless and would likely have caused the escape party some considerable inconvenience. Seeking refuge in a peasant's home, the group settled down for a night's sleep, made easier by the copious amount of vodka they had consumed that day.

Refreshed in the morning, they strapped their boots into the skis and began their journey. For the next three days the party skied across the mountains of Slovakia, constantly heading east towards Poland. Jaksch's biographer Martin Bachstein noted that the group were "not practiced winter sportsmen" and in particular Jaksch, who having broken his leg recently in a car crash, put in "an incredible performance."[124] They would ski almost non-stop for 12 hours each day, from sunrise before 6 a.m. through to dusk at 6 p.m.. As darkness would descend over the mountains, Kminek and his group would plead with any locals they would come across to allow them shelter for the night from the elements. During the daytime, temperatures would reach a comfortable $10°^C$ but then rapidly drop off to freezing when the sun went down.

For the first two days, their skiing was uninterrupted and they were never stopped or questioned on the almost completely abandoned mountains. However on the third day, as the Polish Frontier neared, they ran into some trouble. The further they headed out of Bohemia, the more open the terrain became, leaving the group of five exposed. At around midday, they skied up a ridge to find a track at the top, which led to what appeared to be a large tourist inn. The ground around the barn-like wooden building was not the untouched white snow they were used to, instead it was dirt brown and clearly well trampled. Concerned that the inn could be a SS station, the escape party agreed that Kminek would go ahead to do a recce alone while the other four remained below the ridge to avoid being seen from the inn. Keeping to the side of the track, Kminek had only been gone for a few minutes before a convoy of military trucks came into view, heading towards the inn.

What Jaksch, Sacher and the two women left behind in the ridge did not realise was that, although hidden from view from view from the inn, they were completely exposed to anyone on the other side, where the trucks were now emerging. Clearly in view of the approaching convoy, the four remained crouched below the ridge as any attempts to hide or run would now be useless. When the lorries were parallel to them Jaksch recalled thinking that "the colourful composition of (his) group seemed to be an advantage (with) two women with bright sweaters and two (ski uniformed) men as the Nazi soldiers waved to them and passed on to the inn."[125] Once the vehicles had come to a halt down the track at the inn, Kminek returned, reporting what the others already knew, that the inn was swarming with SS, on their way to reinforce the Polish border.

With no other option, the group of five simply inserted their snow shoes into their ski bindings and headed past the inn and on towards Poland. This was now the second time Jaksch had come face-to-face with German soldiers, without any suspicion. As he passed some soldiers, he imagined them thinking "how beautiful the Czechs have (life)" unaware the value one of these skiers was worth if captured.[126]

Although they had once again come eye-to-eye with the advancing Nazis, the group knew they were far from safe. The convoy of trucks now parked behind them at the inn would soon be on the move again, and as they were also heading to the Polish frontier, they would likely be right behind the ski party.

For the remainder of the third day on the slopes, the party pushed forward relentlessly. As they entered the last few hours of their journey, "the tiredness (of the day) made itself felt."[127] Food supplies were now completely empty and energy levels were rapidly falling. Sacher, the oldest of the group, began to fall behind and break away from the rest of the group. A long sufferer of cardiac troubles, the strain was becoming too much for him.

Kimek knew that the SS soldiers would be fast approaching them, having the more efficient mode of motorised transport to their advantage. The skiing party were leaving tracks, impossible to conceal, but easy to follow if needed. Now was not the time for the group to slow down. They tried their hardest to encourage Sacher, knowing that they were only a matter of hours away from the Polish border, but every time they would start to regain momentum, they "heard from below his pleading voice not to leave him behind."[128]

The final hours of the day were therefore considerably sluggish, but the group agreed they must remain together and all cross the border as one, or be caught as one. They decided to deviate from the open slopes into the dense forests, knowing that the SS convoy behind would be less likely to follow them through such tough terrain. Dusk was fast approaching and navigation was becoming tough. Fortune was on their side, as they stumbled across a bemused Slovak forest worker, "who agreed to take them to the Polish border" for a small sum of money.[129]

By this point, they were getting "slower and slower" but the journey they knew was nearly over.[130] Their new guide took them deeper and deeper into the forest, before holding his hand up and bringing the group to a halt. He pointed to "the marked spot on the trunk (of a tree) and said 'here is Poland.'"[131]

Their remarkable three day journey had ended in the most unremarkable way. With visions of high barbed-wire fences, border guards and menacing German Shepherds, the group were surprised, albeit in a positive way, that they had been able to simply pass a marked tree trunk and were now out of Nazi occupied land.

This was not the time for celebration, as they were well aware that border guards on either side could still make their efforts be in vain. They pushed on until it was completely dark, settling in a small town, Bohumín, which the Poles had recently occupied. Exhausted, they found a tiny inn who were able to accommodate the five of them.

Kminek sent off a telegram to Warriner saying "Montag in Bohumín."[132] This was the signal which Warriner had been waiting for. She booked herself on the overnight train to Bohumín, with a bag packed with the passports, visas and entry permits required to get the five escapers through Poland and on to Britain – the final hurdle needed to get Jaksch out of harm's way. She wrote "the object of my journey was to hand over their passports."[133]

Warriner knew that her journey could jeopardize the whole operation, especially by this point when she was becoming known to the Gestapo. She therefore bribed the train guard at Wilson Station to keep her sleeper cabin door locked for the whole journey, which he did. The next morning she emerged from Bohumín Station to be greeted by five exhausted but relieved people: "As I walked out of the station, a skiing party of three men and two women, brown and dirty and very fit, came across the street to meet me."[134] They spent the day recounting the ordeal they had been through, describing it as "three days of exhaustion" and exchanging the necessary documentation, destroying the fakes.[135] She saw Jaksch and the others off, as they headed for their well-deserved freedom in Britain and returned to Prague on the night train, arriving early on 28th March.

On the day of her arrival, she was greeted into a slightly clearer Prague by Stopford, who was bearing news. He had managed to negotiate with the Gestapo the safe release of those seven still being held up at the Legation, on the condition that they hand over Jaksch and if so, they would imprison him in a location of his choosing. The Gestapo now correctly knew that he had been held at the Legation. After some shouting and screaming from the Gestapo leaders when they were told that Jaksch had escaped, under the noses of their men stationed outside, they honoured their word to Stopford, allowing Taub, his wife and the others to leave that day safely by air to Poland and then on to Sweden.

CHAPTER 16

THE CRACKDOWN

"Demoralise the enemy from within by surprise, terror, sabotage,
assassination. This is the war of the future."
Adolf Hitler[136]

By 30th March, there were signs of yet more trouble to come. News arrived to Warriner that some of the women had been refused exit visas and would only be granted them if they were to go to the newly established Gestapo Headquarters in Prague personally. Another woman had been present when three locals were brutally beaten, arrested and taken away from the hotel they were hiding in. They were getting more and more worried and rightly so, as they were in greater danger every day they remained hidden.

Warriner understood that she had to get them out within days, to avoid them being discovered, so booked them all onto the 11 p.m. train leaving the next evening. She decided that to use a similar tactic Gilles had employed earlier in the month could be the best way. What she needed to now do was get exit visas for them all and also, somehow, persuade the authorities to allow those without passports to go as well. Having consulted Chadwick on this, they agreed that this simply wouldn't be possible, so instead they decided to give anyone without a passport a fake which will have belonged to women who had not turned up or crossed the border illegally. At about 9 p.m. on 31st March, having spent the previous hour with Chadwick packing supplies for the women, they arrived at Wilson Station. There were 70 women and children present, who were to be escorted by Dougan for the journey, meaning 30 people had not arrived and were therefore unaccounted for at this point. Warriner and Chadwick assumed that, similar to last train to leave, they had very little time to get to the station and would most likely be on their way. They could be put on a train the following day if they were not to arrive in time.

With no more people showing up by 11 p.m., Chadwick and Warriner could do nothing but stand back and wave off the group of 70 now on board the train. As the carriages began to strain out of the platform, there was a huge commotion from behind the guard hut, and the train suddenly screeched to a halt, having only moved a few yards. Then five or six large men sprinted down the platform, flinging doors open, banging on windows and ordering people out of the train. Dragged from their seats, all the passengers were searched on the platform, including babies and young children. All bags were emptied and the belongings kicked across the platform. Every passport was checked, but amazingly none of the fake ones were noticed. A woman was grabbed from the group and placed on a bench alone, surrounded by some of the men towering over her. A few minutes later, a man was also pulled from the group, with his wife screaming frantically after him, and placed next to the woman. Not standing for this, Warriner and Chadwick stepped forward and approached the man who looked like he was in charge.

"Who are you?" Warriner demanded, firmly prodding the man on the back of his shoulder, so he swung round aggressively.

"Secret State Police," he retorted moodily, pulling a badge from his pocket. "Passport," he ordered.[137]

Warriner produced hers from her pocket and handed it to him. He then spent the next five minutes looking through it page by page, comparing the picture with her face time and again, before supposedly checking the authenticity of it in the light. Luckily they had not been so detailed with their checks of the women on the train. He then turned on Chadwick, who told them they were together and handing over his documents for the same scrutiny. He grunted and handed them both back their passports.

"This woman has a visa for England," Warriner insisted, gesturing to the shivering figure perched on the bench. "And she has an exit permit signed by the Gestapo themselves," she persevered. As they tried to speak, she went on, "Why can't she leave?"[138]

The response was simple, with the chief saying "the Gestapo gives no information," and turning back to tormenting the woman, calling her, "Communist muck," and the man a "dirty Jew."[139]

As for Warriner and Chadwick, they were completely helpless. There was nothing they could say to these German officers. There was no logic behind their search and no reason why they chose that one man and woman. There were many others on the train who were Jewish and even more were Communists among the women. But all they could do was to stand back and hope the train would be able to leave. Warriner wanted to get a message to Dougan, to tell her to get the women with fake documents off the train as soon as possible, knowing that it would be searched at every station from here to the border, and once there, the real trouble would start. But with State Secret Police all around, searching under the train, having it moved back and forward, shouting all around, there was no way to sneak over. Dougan herself was getting an earful from the men, calling her "the lying and traitorous English." [140] Eventually, after hours of this brutality and terror the train departed early in the morning of 1st April. The man left at the bench was taken away and no record of him exists. The woman, Wanda Bauernfeind, who was known to Warriner, was taken away and never heard of again. She had just turned 25 that month.

***

Warriner made her way back to The Alcron Hotel, weary and scared following their ordeal. After a few hours' sleep, which was becoming quite normal for her by this point, she was awoken with a message that Adi Kolarik, secretary of the Sudeten Communist party had been arrested. She had been caught the previous day as she had left her hiding place to try and inform the thirty missing women that the train was leaving that evening, explaining why they had not showed up the night before. Adi was extremely determined, and had been a huge help to Warriner over the past month in Prague since the Nazis had arrived. She had put her own safety second, to try and help the others. She was taken to a concentration camp and was presumed to have been killed there.

Later that morning, Warriner had a call from Dougan at the Legation. This was a worry, as she was meant to be in Poland with the 70 woman on the train from the night before. She explained that she had the same concern as Warriner and had decided to take those with fake passports off the train when it stopped at a signal, getting on a return train back to Wilson station.

One of the women, Elisabeth Baier, was heavily pregnant with her fifth child and not in a good way. They decided to take her to a safe house that Warriner was using to house lost children and the most vulnerable. The house belonged to a Jewish lady called Ruza Erhmannová, who had agreed to loan it to Warriner for as long as she needed it, on condition she helped her two children to escape the country. On Easter Sunday, Baier miscarried and was rushed to hospital, where she only just survived.

During the start of April, Warriner, Chadwick and Stopford worked tirelessly to continue to get the neccssary exit visas for those still left. These were the women and children who had their passports lost and the 30 who had not received the message in time to board the last train on the night of the 31st

March. They were able to slowly get the necessary exit papers, but only really one at a time. One woman who had been waiting for months was Marie Greiss.

To her delight, her Polish travel visa finally arrived and the Nazis had granted her an exit permit. It turned out that the Polish had spelt her name on the visa with a "z" at the end rather than "ss." Warriner pleaded with the Polish authorities to rectify their mistake, but they insisted on getting written confirmation from London. This further delay was one of many blows Marie had encountered since she fled the Sudetenland, and she was gutted when Warriner broke the news that she would need to wait. When the message did come from London a few days later that she would be accepted, the Poles were happy and Warriner called Marie to pass her the good news. She was unable to reach her, even after searching for her for several days. Marie could not face it anymore. She had been promised on too many occasions that she would be allowed to leave, to only be told at the last minute she was no longer able to. She lost all hope and did not believe she would ever be able to leave and be reunited with her husband. Her friend found her three days later. She had hanged herself.

***

Warriner was becoming in increasing personal danger. Her phone was now tapped, which she could tell from "the more sinister re-echo" she would hear when she made calls.[141] Clearly involved in illegal activity, she was well aware that not only was she in danger, but the women and children she was helping were also coming into the spotlight. The BCRC was now tangled in a web of underground activity that the Gestapo were becoming furious about. She also received news following the raid on her old office. Chadwick was having one of his regular meetings with the Gestapo chiefs, and the topic of Warriner's office came up. They stated how disappointed and surprised they had been with what they had found, claiming that although it was known her work had been underhand, they were shocked and confused by her activities. Chadwick was becoming increasingly worried that she had left details of the underground work they were doing, or worse, the whereabouts of the women hiding in hotels around the city had somehow been discovered.

In fact, they had found something much more peculiar. Pornography… and lots of it. There were bookshelves all around Warriner's office, filled with thick, red, leather-bound books containing German pornography. The building in which the BCRC had requisitioned for their headquarters used to belong to a publishing company, who were not an everyday publishers. They were focused on post World War I erotic photography. Warriner had adopted one of their storerooms as an office, which happened to be surrounded by a lot of stock. She had asked on several occasions for these to be removed, but given the hype of activity, this soon fell to the bottom of the priority list.

Warriner decided that she would not mention this story to her counterparts in London. After her last visit and dressing down she had about her comments to the press, she was already on very thin ice. A scandal of this nature could tip her over the edge and plus Chadwick agreed to keep this quiet as well. The

Gestapo were trying to spread the story around the city, through Chadwick and others, but it was so bizarre that no-one really took any notice. The officers did take away many of the books for thorough examination, checking them page by page in the privacy of their own rooms, apparently to make sure there were no messages hidden within – one of their more enjoyable tasks that winter.

On 14th April, the Gestapo stormed the hostel where many of the BCRC workers were staying. It was 6 a.m. and the whole city was dark and silent, apart from the shouting and smashing of the Germany officers who were disturbing the peace. They were looking for Warriner, mistaking her instead for Beatrice Wellington as she looked very similar, whom they arrested. Wellington was part of the Quakers movement who recently travelled from Canada to help the Czech people and had subsequently started to work for the BCRC. She was bundled into the back of a car, straight from her bed where she had been sleeping. In the room opposite hers had been Maxwell and Dougan, who were in a lot more danger than Wellington as they were actively involved with the illegal work. Maxwell in particular was being searched for, as the Gestapo had arrested a wanted Sudeten man who had her card in his pocket, with a small wad of cash wrapped around it.

Luckily, they thought Wellington was their woman and did not think to search the rest of the hostel in their excitement. Wellington was driven to the Germans' office on Perštýn Street, where she was intensely questioned. Third Reich expert, author and lecturer, Frank McDonough, explained that "every arrested person who entered a Gestapo office was fingerprinted and photographed."[142] Although it is likely Wellington was not an exception, no photographs have been found in Gestapo archives. It was at this point they realised they had arrested the wrong woman, but decided she could still be a useful source of information.

McDonough went on to say "the key part of all Gestapo investigations was the interrogation (where) the accused person was asked to answer a series of questions."[143] As was common practice for the Gestapo interrogators, they made Wellington stand through the whole ordeal, while firing questions at her without a breath, answering the questions themselves before she had a chance to respond. This lasted a few hours, until they were mildly satisfied, and let her leave. They told her that they would be picking her up again the next morning for further questioning. They had repeatedly asked for details her about Maxwell and Dougan and in particular their whereabouts.

Wellington returned to the Legation where, exhausted after her ordeal although physically unharmed, she informed the authorities of the imminent danger of Maxwell and Dougan. The Legation took the warning seriously, insisting on their immediate departure. Wellington was not seen to be in the same danger, as she had been released by the Gestapo and genuinely did not know about the illegal activity the others were involved in. With some literal kicking and screaming, Maxwell and Dougan were taken to Wilson Station that evening, catching the 11 p.m. train away from danger.

The next morning, on 15th April, an official from the British Consulate arrived at 6 a.m. outside Wellington's hostel to accompany her back to the Gestapo offices for further questioning. Wellington had been told to arrive at 7 a.m. that morning, and it had been decided that it would be safest for her to go accompanied by an official. He waited outside the hostel for some time, before heading inside to wake her up believing she had overslept. He found her room abandoned, the bed unmade and the blinds still drawn. With a huge amount of concern, the official raced back to the Legation to sound the alarm.

For the whole morning, officials drove from Nazi office to Nazi office, searching for Wellington. At this early point in the German invasion, some of the diplomatic laws were abided by, giving the representatives from the Legation and Consulate the ability to question the whereabouts of Wellington. Chadwick and Stopford used their network within the Gestapo, but to no avail. Unsuccessful, the search party returned to the Legation at around midday, in a state of shock having not been able to find her. As they entered the building, they were confronted by a familiar face. It was the person they had been searching for all morning.

Wellington had in fact been in one of the Gestapo offices just outside Prague and not within the search radius of her attempted rescuers. Officers had woken her in the early hours of that morning, dragging her from her bed to a car. Once in their offices, they fired questions at her for six hours, again forcing her to stand throughout the ordeal. She later discovered that she had been taken, in Stopford's words, "by the dreaded Sicherheitsdienst."[144] Shortened to the SD, this was the deadly intelligence agency of the Nazis, which being led by Reinhard Heydrich until his assassination by a British lead team on 27th May 1942, for which "Czech civilians were to pay the price."[145]

Wellington was not someone who was afraid of confrontation and by all accounts she stood up the SD officers magnificently. They were in fact a different group of soldiers all together to those who had taken her the day before.

Such questions and answers would go as follows, with them asking, "where is the British Legations?"[146]

"Look in the telephone book" Wellington bravely responded.[147]

They went on to accuse her of hiding many of the women they were looking for in the Legation, which Wellington denied. Their knowledge was fairly accurate, as although the women were not actually being hidden in the Legation itself, but rather by those inside. Wellington could quite honestly say she had no knowledge of this, which was the truth. They told her that none of the women would be allowed to leave the country unless they were to meet with a Gestapo official, who would try and talk sense into them to return to their "home" the Sudetenland. They were clearly furious and bewildered why a group of Aryan German women would want to go anywhere but to Nazi territory.

As the interrogation was coming to an end, the officers accused her of illegal activity, to which she said: "everything that you do is illegal."[148]

Once they were done with her, she made her own way back to the Legation where she was met by a group of shocked colleagues, who she discovered had been out looking for her most of the morning. Like the previous day, she was not in any physical harm, however she was understandably exhausted by the morning's interrogations. It was suggested that she may be in too much danger and that she should leave, but Wellington quickly pointed out that she was not the one they were really looking for and flatly refused to go anywhere. Once composed and after lots of coffee and something to eat, she turned her attention to the women that she had been questioned about so ferociously. Wellington, Stopford, Warriner and Chadwick discussed the predicament the women were now in. Although the Nazis did not know exactly where they were, they did know that they were still in the country and that they were being hidden by a refugee organisation.

The only option, Stopford explained, would be for all the women and children still on the list, which was now just 120, to give their addresses to the Gestapo and allow them to be visited. This was not something which Warriner felt she could decide on their behalf, so on 16th April she set off to all the hiding places of the women and children. At each, she put the question to them: 'would you like me to give the Gestapo your address?' Although it may seem like the only answer would be no, if the women would not be visited, then Stopford would have no chance of getting them exit visas.

All the women trusted Warriner by this point, as they all agreed to have their addresses given to the Nazis and would allow themselves to be met by officers. Their safety was only assured as they themselves were not accused of any anti-Nazi crimes, were White Aryans and had the safety blanket of Stopford wrapped around them. Warriner told each of the women that they should not believe any of the propaganda they would be told about returning to the 'fatherland.' She feared that some of the women had spent so long in ghettos that their exhaustion would mean they could cave in under the pressure.

What followed were two days of visits by the Kriminalrat and some of his assistants to several of the addresses. They spilled endless propaganda to the women, promising them and their children the world and beyond. They also assured them complete personal safety. When one of the women enquired what would happen if her husband, a known socialist, was to return with her, she was told that he would not have the same assurance. Taking Warriner's advice, all the women refused to believe any of the promises or threats. After visiting the first two addresses on their list, the Kriminalrat and his helpers gave up, knowing it was a lost cause.

Upon their return to their office, following what was a very unsuccessful morning for them, the Gestapo group were greeted by Stopford. He was waiting for them to honour their word of passing over the passports and exit documents. Quite surprisingly they handed over all the identifications as they had promised, totalling 80. As Stopford was turning to leave with eighty passports stuffed into a bag, the Kriminalrat called him to one side. He passed on a warning that Warriner should leave the country immediately. He produced a card, signed by Warriner, addressed to the Consul in Katowice, a city in Southwestern Poland. The card had been found in the possession of a wanted political refugee who had been arrested after attempting to escape the country across the Polish border.

Warriner argued against the legitimacy of this note, however she did concede that her remaining could severely damage the rescue operation. After consulting with Stopford, Wellington and Chadwick, she agreed that her only option would be to return to Britain. Beatrice Wellington and Trevor Chadwick were both more than capable and willing to take over the role in its entirety. In true Warriner form, she decided that there was no time to waste and that she should be the one to escort another transport from the country.

So off she went, tying up loose ends. She visited all the hotels holding the remaining women, ordering those whose passports had been returned to Stopford to meet her at Wilson Station in time for the now very familiar 11 p.m. train to Ostrava. Back on the terrace of the Legation she and Chadwick discussed the next steps for the children's section he was running with Winton. The children she still had under her care would now be looked after by Chadwick, until the next transport was organised. There was just time for her and Wellington to put the final pieces of the jigsaw in place for that evening's transport and off to the station they went, the last time for Warriner.

They were greeted by the eighty women and children as well as several Gestapo officers, who were shouting and generally causing concern to the passengers. When Warriner arrived, the officers quickly turned their attention to her. They gave her a quick cross examination about her alliance with the Jewish firm Čedok and snatched the bag she was carrying which contained all eighty passports. As they began to sift through them, Warriner mentioned that Stopford was on his way and she was sure he would be able to answer any of their questions.

Showing the power of Stopford's reputation by this point, the Gestapo officers immediately handed back the passports and stopped their shouting. In what would be her final interaction with the Nazis of Prague, Warriner complained that they had returned the passports disarranged from the alphabetical order they had been in and asked for an apology, which they were happy to give. She then turned her back on them and ordered the women onto the train. At 11p.m., like clockwork, the train steamed out of the station. Warriner sat in a compartment looking out of the window. The dark city started to race away from her. All she was thinking about were those she had left behind.

At 5 a.m. on 23rd April, their train entered the safety of the Polish frontier. They spent several days in Poland, travelling between Krakow and Katowice, where Warriner had friends she stayed with. On 28th April, they boarded the boat in Gdynia and headed for the shores of Britain.

Back in Prague, just a handful of women and children remained, with Wellington taking over the duties of Warriner and with Chadwick and Stopford busily dealing with the Gestapo. True to their word to Warriner that they would get the remaining families out, on 22nd May, the train carrying the last of the 40 remaining family members arrived at Liverpool Street to be greeted by Warriner.

CHAPTER 17

CHILDREN

*"I shall always have a feeling of shame that I didn't
get more (children) out."*
Trevor Chadwick[149]

The departure of Warriner certainly left a void for Chadwick
and the others at the BCRC. She had been a constant for them
all, while everything else had been so uncertain.

From his time in the country, Chadwick had been
supporting the work of the BCRC in all the ways he could. But
his main remit was to look after the Children's Section for the
country. For the start of 1939, he had been adding names to the
list of 760 people whom he and Winton had returned to
London with at the beginning of January. The list now had over
6,000 names of children on it. We know this because Winton
was quoted in the Newcastle Evening Chronicle, "Mr Nicholas
Winton (said) he had 6,000 children on his books waiting to be
brought to this country."[150] By this point, he had only managed
to arrange up to five plane loads of twenty children and then
one trainload of a further twenty children to leave. This caused
him some considerable desperation.

Nevertheless, he and Winton worked tirelessly to arrange for the next transport to leave. They were not able to work at the same speed as Warriner had with the adult section, as the new strict measures the occupying Nazis had implemented meant that their process was tiresome and tedious.

As the month of April began, they were nearly ready for their second trainload to leave. Over the next month, they would arrange for three trains to leave carrying a total of 126 children out of Czechoslovakia. The first arrived in London Liverpool Street on 19th April, three days before Chadwick's 32nd birthday, with a train of 36 children aboard on, followed quickly on 29th April with 29 children and then on 13th May, the largest up to that point, with 61 children aboard. The latter train's passengers were all unknowingly travelling with forged documents. Chadwick recalled that he "could wait no longer" as he had "guarantors lined up and the children waiting," so decided to take matters into his own hands. Using his growing underground network he "had some (visas) made, as near as possible like the Home Office ones."[151] This incredibly risky tactic did pay off and no official was suspicious of the documents, allowing the children to safely travel through Germany before swapping the fakes "for the tardy but valid Home Office permits," according to Winton's daughter.[152]

So far, the operation was clearly quite an achievement for Winton and Chadwick, who had managed what many had failed in – bringing unaccompanied children into Britain from Czechoslovakia. However, they both knew that the pace of the recue needed to pick up, as they had only brought a tiny fraction of those they had on their books.

They managed to increase the pace with the next group leaving just under a month later, on 2nd June with 123 children, nearly doubling the total number of children evacuated. This train also had a special guest on board – none other than Trevor Chadwick. Exactly why he left at this point of the operation is not entirely known, although he recalled that "in the evenings there were other fish to fry which did not have anything to do with the children. It became obvious to me as summer developed that certain of my movements were at least suspect, and that (Bömelburg) and his boys might turn sour." [153] Concerned that this might impact the safety of the children he "explained these things to London and they arranged a replacement."[154]

His son, William, has several theories as to why he decided to leave, including an involvement in underground forgeries, hoodwinking with the Gestapo or spying for the British. All explanations are plausible, especially the suggestion that he was spying for the British. As William Chadwick points out, "it would have been amazing if Chadwick... had not been approached by MI6" given his close working relationship with senior Nazi officials.[155] Whatever the reason, a letter sent from Wellington in Prague to Layton in London dated at the beginning of June started with the line: "I am taking advantage of Chadwick's journey to send you this."[156]

One of the infants on this train with Chadwick was Tom Schrecker, aged just seven. His uncle, Frank Schrecker, had already fled to London after the Munich Agreement and had spent several months desperately trying to help his nephew get to safety. For several days, he would queue at the refugee centre in London, trying to see who could help. Sadly, there were hundreds of people ahead of him in the queue, all trying in vain to do the same.

He eventually decided to take drastic action, so dressed in a suit and carrying a briefcase as a prop, he walked straight through the reception, confidently heading to the offices. Not speaking any English, he looked for any Czech-sounding names written on the endless doors. Eventually finding one, he knocked and entered a small office to find two women chatting. They initially tried to send him away, but he produced a photo of Tom and pleaded with them for help. As luck would have it, one of these ladies was Jean Barbour, who immediately offered to take Tom into her home. Just before leaving Prague, Tom's father had arranged for him to be baptised as a Roman Catholic, as an extra precaution and also likely at the suggestion of Jean Barbour.

Jean met the train as it arrived on the morning 3rd June, along with guardians of the other 122 children. From information she had been given by Tom's father, Jean knew that Tom was a huge animal lover and so the first stop from Liverpool Street Station was London Zoo. From there, they drove to Jean's home in Oxford, where her other two adopted children awaited the arrival of their new "brother" with excitement. Known as Marnie by her "children", she went on to adopt a fourth child, the three-year-old son of a Polish fighter pilot, killed in the Battle of Britain.

Back in Prague, Tom's mother, Markéta, was one of the millions to be sent to an "unknown destination" and never seen or heard of again. She had remained in Prague to care for her sick mother, having divorced Tom's father, with whom Tom was living until his departure to Britain. Tom was one of only a handful of the children who came to England to ever see one of his parents again. His father, Robert, had been arrested for making anti-Nazi comments, following a tip-off from one of his disgruntled employees and sent to Pankrác prison. Quite remarkably, his secretary marched into the Gestapo headquarters in the capital and told them that the accusations were false and demanded his release. What was even more amazing, it worked. He was freed after two months of imprisonment on the condition that he handed over his business to the Nazis, which he of course did. After his release, he fled to China through Italy, where he stayed for the duration before heading to Britain where he was reunited with his brother and son. Although he was only imprisoned for two months, the toll on him was great, turning his hair completely grey in that period.

The largest of the transports contained 241 children, arriving in Liverpool Street on 1ˢᵗ July, a month after the previous train. The children had left Prague at around midnight on 30ᵗʰ June, waved off by hundreds of family members, by far the largest farewell party of the operation. The children were able to pass through German occupied Czechoslovakia, into Germany without any bother, until they reached the border. As normal, the Germans decided to search the train. The police walked through the carriages, emptying each child's suitcase onto the floor, kicking the contents around to check for any contraband, then moving on to the next suitcase.

Despite the train being in considerable disorder and mess after this affair, the train passed into Holland safely. They were greeted by locals handing out cheese sandwiches and hot coco, talking endlessly in Dutch to children, who nodded along obligingly, not understanding a word said to them but grateful for the substance and kindness. They arrived at London Liverpool Street late on 1st July, to all be greeted by their new foster parents.

Although no one knew at the time, the penultimate train left Prague on 19th July with 76 children on board heading for Holland and eventually Britain. One of the children travelling was sixteen-year-old Mimka Klímová, one of the eldest to travel on the seven trains. She had been booked on the previous journey, however the only sponsor left wanted a girl who was between the age of ten and fourteen. Mimka's ten-year-old sister, Alice, took her place instead. As we have already seen, this operation left the children's fate purely in the hands of luck

The final train departed from Prague on 2nd August with only 66 out of the planned 68 children on board, having to make a stop in Germany to collect eleven-year-old Joe Schlesignger and his nine-year-old brother from Lovosice Station, inside the German Reich. The two boys were forced to wait with their father in the men's toilet at the station, as Jews were not permitted to enter waiting rooms. With a full load, the train then travelled through Germany, taking a lot longer than the other trains, arriving at the Dutch border only to have their train and possessions endlessly searched by the German police. It was to their great relief that they were allowed through, also being greeted by the Dutch serving them hot coco and white bread – something most of the children had never eaten before. Some children described it as tasting wet or like cotton wool, while some threw it out of the window.

The train arrived at the Hook of Holland, where they boarded a large steam boat, heading for the safety of the British coast. The overnight voyage was slow, but the children were exhausted and were able to sleep, being rocked by the English Channel waves. They then boarded their final train early in the morning, heading for London Liverpool Street. The Schlesignger brothers were actually greeted by Winton's mother, who took them to her flat where they stayed before being collected by their foster parents.

Another two of the 68 children were bothers Hugo and Rudy Maron, aged eleven and nine at the time. Their arrival was less seamless than the Schlesignger children, as for some reason there was no one waiting to collect them. The brothers waited for hours on the station platform, with no one asking if they were okay – quite strange when you think there were nearly two children waiting unattended. It was only when a taxi driver stopped to ask them if they were okay, were offered help. They explained that their guardian, named Mr Rabinowitz, was due to pick them up, but they had no details for him.

The taxi driver kindly took them to a fish and chip shop for some food, the first they had had since they were in Holland. He then let them stay with his family for a couple of days before finding them an orphanage in Cricklewood, where they stayed for a several weeks, before being collected by some newly-assigned foster parents. Fortunately, the other 66 children were collected at the station as planned, however this story does demonstrate the challenge which was still faced by Winton on the British side of the operation, even after the children were able to escape.

Another child on this train, Josef Ginat, was adopted by a Christian minister who was waiting for him at the station. There were many stories of Christian's adopting Jewish children, in the hope that they could convert them, or in some cases, only adopting children who had been baptised into the Christian church. The minister who looked after Josef did the opposite. He adapted part of his church to resemble a synagogue, and bought as much Jewish merchandise as he could lay his hands on, saying "I pray in my way, so you should pray in your way."[157]

On 1st September 1939, a train carrying 250 children, the largest group yet, was cancelled hours before it was due to leave Prague as a result of Germany's invasion of Poland which pulled Britain into WWII. The fate of these 250 children is not known, except for a few who were able escape by other means. The others are most likely to have been sent to Theresienstadt and on to Auschwitz where their fate was devastatingly predictable.

CHAPTER 18

LOOSE ENDS

"Some are born great, some achieve greatness...
some have greatness thrust upon them."
William Shakespeare

Hitler's advance into Poland in September 1939 not only signalled the start of another World War in the space of 25 years, but also meant the end of any further significant rescue work from Czechoslovakia. The BCRC's operations in Prague were disbanded on 21st July 1939 and was morphed into the newly formed the Czech Refugee Trust Fund (CRTF). The CRTF "assumed all the responsibilities and liabilities previously administered by the BCRC" according to academic Dr Martin D. Brown, which was to "oversee the distribution of the £3.5 million that remained" from the British loan. [158] Culpin remained as one of the three trustees of the organisation.

Of the children rescued under the BCRC, around 700 in total, their descendants at the time of writing today number over 6,000, none of whom would exist today had it not been for those written about.

Vera Gissing, the 10-year-old who escaped thanks to Winton and Chadwick's efforts, went on to be an established writer. A lot of her work was related to her youth, with her most successful being her autobiography called *Pearls of Childhood*, published in 1988 and continued in prominence to now, where it has recently been released in its eighth edition. She has also worked with Slovakian film director Matej Minac on several films about Nicholas Winton, while also never stopping her campaigning for Holocaust education.

On train number eight, Joseph Ginat moved from Britain after the war to Israel and began a successful career as an engineer. Huge Maron from the same train went on to become a pilot before retiring as an airport designer, having designed Paraguay International Airport among many others. Also on this last train was Joe Schlesignger, who became a well-known journalist, reporting on conflicts in Indochina, Vietnam, Pakistan, Nicaragua, El Salvador, Afghanistan and Iraq.

One of the three children who Trevor Chadwick and Geoff Phelps collected to go to Forres School, Gerda Mayer, went on to become a leading poet, described by Poet Laureate Carole Ann Duffy as someone "who should be better known."[159]

A whole book could be dedicated to the lives of those saved within this story, and it is not possible to go into detail on all.

A man who was both a rescuer and rescued was Wenzel Jaksch. After escaping to Britain, Jaksch continued to fight for the rights of Sudeten Germans. He also began a long running feud with Edvard Beneš, President of Czechoslovakia in exile, at the time living in Buckinghamshire, having withdrawn from his home in Putney during the Blitz. After the war, Beneš was able to persuade the British Government not to allow Jaksch back to Western Germany, because "Jaksch demanded a strict separation of Czech and German regions and even proposed a transfer of national minorities."[160] This ban was only lifted in 1949, a year after Beneš had died in 1948 of poor health following a series of strokes that year.

Upon his return to Germany, Jaksch became the second President of the Federation of Expellees in Germany, replacing its former president Hans Krüger, forced to step down for having Nazi links. The organisation was set up to represent the interests of Germans expelled during the previous two conflicts.

Jaksch was killed in a road accident in 1966 aged 70. A fate which he had narrowly avoided in 1938 before his first meetings with Warriner, Gilles and Grenfell, where he had escaped a car crash with only a broken leg. Sadly, details of the metal worker, Kminek, the elderly Sacher and the two women who had put everything on the line to help Jaksch escape persecution in Prague, are non-existent.

Prior to his death, Jaksch had presented Grenfell with a thanksgiving painting by Czech artist Ernst Neuschel, one of the men who the BCRC had helped to escape Prague, in recognition of his efforts. During the war, Grenfell acted as Chairman of the Welsh Parliamentary Labour Party and joined Churchill's coalition government as Secretary for Mines at the Board of Trade.

After the war, Grenfell was sworn in as a Privy Councillor in 1951, before becoming "Father of the House" in 1953. This latter title is for someone "who has (continuously) served longer in the House of Commons than any other MP,"[161] a title which would have been given to Winston Churchill had he not broken his time as a MP in 1922 when he lost his seat. Grenfell died at his home in Swansea aged 87 in 1968, outliving Jaksch by two years.

The other Labour Party MP with Grenfell from the start, William Gillies had a less celebrated career in politics. Although he served 25 years as International Secretary of the Labour Party, he was dismissed in 1944. According to Warriner, he became "well known for his strongly anti-Communist and anti-German views" which caused a lot of upset to German Sudeten refugees, such as Jaksch.[162] Exactly why his views changed so drastically from 1938 having personally helped so many Germans to escape persecution is not known. He was an adamant supporter of the theory of Vansittartism, "the assertion that Nazism was a product of specifically German tradition and culture," which eventually led to his dismissal, accused of misleading the views of the Labour Party.[163] He died aged 73 in 1958.

Eleanor Rathbone remained an independent MP until her death one year after the end of the war in 1946 aged 73. Despite dying before many of the other politicians involved in this story, she was still able to see the Family Allowance Act pass into law in 1945. She is credited for pioneering this act, which was the first ever child benefit law for Britain.

Joint Vice-Chairman with Grenfell on the Parliamentary Committee on Refugees, which Rathbone had founded and sat as Honouree Secretary, was Arthur Salter. Appointed a Privy Counsellor in 1941, Salter remained as MP for Oxford University until 1950 before taking the seat as MP for Ormskirk. He was appointed as Minister of State for Economic Affairs under the new Chancellor of Exchequer Rab Butler in

1951 when Churchill resumed his premiership of Britain. In justifying Salter's appointment, Churchill described him as "the greatest economist since Jesus Christ."[164] He died in 1975 aged 94, by which point he was Baron Salter.

Chairman of the Parliamentary Committee for Refugees Victor Cazalet went on to be Political Liaison Officer Polish Prime Minister Władysław Sikorski. Cazalet was killed on 4th July 1943 aged 47 in an airplane crash, when flying with Sikorski in a "disaster on (the) way home from Gibraltar," according to the Gloucestershire Echo.[165] The accident has been the source of much conspiratorial speculation. Sikorski was one of the Polish officials Robin Hankey, who had met Warriner in Warsaw just after the establishment of the BCRC, had helped to escape the Nazi invasion in 1939.

Hankey himself escaped Warsaw after the arrival of the Nazis and settled in Romania. In 1943, he accompanied Churchill to Tehran to meet with Stalin and Roosevelt, where it is believed that the Allied invasion of France was agreed. After the war he was sent by Churchill to act like a "patient sulky pig" in Egypt during the Suez crisis, before retiring in Stockholm where he died in 1996.[166]

Harold "Gibby" Gibson, known to Warriner as the Passport Control Officer, but unbeknown to her a British intelligence officer, helped ten Czech intelligence officers to fly to London to escape the Nazis in Prague. For this, he was placed on a special 'wanted list' by the SS, who were to prioritise his arrest if Britain was successfully invaded. The leader of these ten Czech agents, František Moravec, went on to plan Operation Anthropoid, the plot to assassinate Reinhard Heydrich.

After the war, Gibson returned to Prague to take up his diplomatic duties, before moving to Berlin and then Rome for work. He was found shot dead in 1960, two years after his retirement, in his flat in Rome. Originally suspected of suicide, it is still not known the exact cause of his death. The plot is further thickened by the fact that Gibson was posthumously suspected of being a Russian mole within MI5.

The eccentric Sir Harold Hales, who had visited the camps in Czechoslovakia with Rathbone and guided by Winton died in 1942 aged 74. Despite being one of the first people recorded to crash an airplane in 1910, his eventual death was less spectacular. According to the Sunderland Daily Echo and Shipping Gazette, Hales accidently "drowned by falling from a boat he was rowing across the Thames."[167]

Chairman of the BCRC Ewart Culpin served as the Labour Party Alderman for London County Council for Battersea North from 1925 until 1946, when he died aged 69.

The man who had appointed Culpin and himself been selected to establish the BCRC, Sir Walter Layton, was drafted into government after war was declared. He held positions within the Ministry of Supply and the Ministry of Production from 1940 until 1942, when he was made Head of Joint Production Staff.

Despite the respect he held in the British political circles, he was a hopelessly unsuccessful politician, losing all three of his attempts to stand for Parliament as a Liberal candidate. He did, however, influence a lot of the population with liberal ideas through his time as Chairman of The Economist and Editor of the News Chronicle. He died aged 81 in 1966; his peerage as

Baron Layton, of Danehill in the County of Sussex was succeeded by the eldest of his seven children.

One of Layton's close friends and business acquaintances was Seebohm Rowntree, the cousin of Tessa Rowntree from the Quakers Movement whom Grenfell had described as "a tough girl"[168] and who accompanied many of Warriner's trains. Tessa went on to marry fellow Quaker and chocolatier tycoon descendant John W. Cadbury in August 1942. After marrying, she continued her philanthropic work, becoming "responsible for the women membership of the Friend's War Relief Service" according to the Yorkshire Evening Post.[169] She died of old age.

Her cousin, Seebohm Rowntree's niece, Jean Rowntree who had worked for the Quakers in Prague with Tessa, died at 97 after a life dedicated to the Quakers.

The Gestapo chief, Karl Bömelburg, was sent to France in 1940 following the Nazi invasion. He lived in a large commune, west of Paris in Neuilly-sur-Seine, in a house which became known as Villa Bömelburg. Highlights under his command included the arrest and killing of hundreds of French Resistance suspects, the regular use of torture in interrogations and helping the German collaborator Philippe Pétain escape to Switzerland after the Allied invasion in 1944.

After the War, Bömelburg reinvented himself as Sergeant Bergman, a German soldier who had died shortly before the Nazi surrender. He was able to effectively forge Bergman's papers, an activity he was familiar with following his time in Prague. Moving to Munich, he worked as a gardener and librarian. A year later, in 1946, he slipped on an icy pavement, fell and died of a head injuries aged 61. Although he never paid

172

for his crimes while alive, he was posthumously sentenced to death by French courts for war crimes. He has yet to be convicted of any crimes in Czechoslovakia.

Father Jozef Tiso, the Slovakian Prime Minister who collaborated with Hitler was sentenced to death in a Czech court in 1947. Tiso's Hlinka Guard, who Jaksch had nearly bumped into while escaping, were responsible for the deaths of thousands of Jews. Slovakia suffered terribly from the Holocaust because of the collaboration with Hitler, with 113,000 Jewish people being killed in the country alone, leaving a population of just 24,000 Jews in 1945.

Konrad Henlein, Jaksch's nemesis in the Sudetenland and leader of the SdP, continued to collaborate with Hitler. After the occupation of Czechoslovakia, he was appointed Reichsstatthalter, Reich Lieutenant, of the Sudetenland and joined the Nazi Party. After the Allies declared victory over the Third Reich in 1945, Henlein was arrested by American soldiers and imprisoned in Czechoslovakia. He died that year, by smashing his eye glasses in his prison cell and using the glass to puncture the arteries in his wrist.

The Liaison Officer, Robert Stopford was flown to America after war was declared with Hitler, taking up a post as Financial Counsellor at the British Embassy in Washington until 1943. At this point he returned to London and joined the War Office as Directorate of Civil Affairs, a post he held until the end of the war. After the war, he was again thrown into deep negotiations, as a member of the Council of Foreign Ministers Boundary Commission, tasked with negotiating the Italian-Yugoslavian territorial disputes.

In later life, Stopford enjoyed his time as a semi-historian, taking a particular interest in Ypres and served as Chairman of the Board of Trustees for the Imperial War Museum. He died aged 83 in 1978.

Sadly, of the "splendidly competent" secretaries who worked tirelessly with Warriner and Chadwick from Prague, little is known. [170] It is with regret that Hilde Patz, Christine Maxwell, Margaret Dougan, and Alois Mollik do not have whole sections of this book about them and all their individual achievements during the rescue operations and in their post-war lives. Despite some extensive research, it has proved too difficult to find out more about their lives. To open this book, the words written by Winton perfectly describe how these four individuals gave up their "time and energy in the alleviation of pain and suffering... finding and helping those who are suffering and in danger."[171] As we have seen throughout this story, without the support of others, Chadwick, Winton and Warriner would never have been able to achieve what they did.

Beatrice Wellington remained in Europe throughout the war, before heading to Poland after the Nazi defeat to provide relief work for the next three years. Ill health forced her to return to America where she unsuccessfully tried to join the U.N. before settling for a teaching role in an Alberta and British Columbia school.

In the winter of 1970, Wellington innocently cut her foot on a piece of glass, which quickly became septic and eventually resulted in being amputated. The surgery proved too much for her body to stand and on 7th April 1971, she died aged 64, having slipped into a coma from which she never awoke.

Our three central characters all slipped back into their separate lives after helping those in Prague. Winton decided against fighting in the war, taking up the stance of a conscience objector, commenting that he "would be willing to help clear up the mess but not take part in the slaughter."[172] Instead, he signed up as a St John Ambulance volunteer, initially setting up Air Raid Precaution centres and then being sent to Calais to help the retreating British Exploration Force in Dunkirk.

The taste of action was enough for him to change his stance, signing up for the RAF in 1941, only to be turned down for his poor eyesight. He was, however, accepted as a flight trainer as part of a pilot training programme.

After the war, Winton joined the Refugee Committee in London where he was posted with two others in Geneva. Travelling 43 times between Germany, France, Switzerland and America in eight months, his role was to liquidate Nazi assets stolen during the holocaust. This involved the collection of anything from jewellery, clothing, and gold fillings from teeth. Winton would collect the loot, have it broken down into basic materials, negotiating the best price for this and then accumulating the money. In total, $25 million was collected and given to support some of those persecuted. Winton would later state that of all his life experiences, this would "stay in (his) memory forever."[173]

Winton then moved to Paris where he met 28-year-old Grete Gjelstrup, whom he went on to marry. The couple had three children, Nick, Barbara, and Robin, who was born with Down Syndrome and died the day before his sixth birthday.

After an early retirement, Winton dedicated his time to various charities, including one for learning disabilities and another for the elderly. This work gained him recognition, culminating in a MBE in 1983. It was not until 1988 that Winton became known to a wider audience for his work in Prague. From that point, his life changed dramatically, as he was rightly given multiple honours for what he achieved, including the freedom of Prague, the Order of Tomas Masaryk, and a knighthood before he died at the incredible age of 106 in 2005.

Such official recognition was not given to Chadwick or Warriner, however both had died around 10 years before the story was ever made known. Despite what was reported in the press, Winton put a lot of energy into giving recognition to the others, in particular Chadwick.

For example, in a letter dated 28th March 1999, Winton wrote "I am delighted to hear that at long last Trevor Chadwick may possibly get full recognition for the part he played in saving children from Czechoslovakia prior to the 2nd World War. I saw the need when I was in Prague, just after Christmas 1938. Trevor came out and offered his help and we set up an office together and he agreed to run the Czech side, if, on my return to England, I was able to make workable arrangements with the Home Office. This I was able to do, and my job then was to find suitable families which fulfilled the Home Office conditions of entry. Trevor then went to work and dealt with all the considerable problems at the Prague end and this work he continued to carry on even when it became more difficult and dangerous when the Germans arrived. He deserves all praise."[174]

Chadwick himself decided on a career in the Royal Navy Reserve, posted on the requisitioned steam yacht H.M.S Mollusc, which was sunk shortly after.

Deciding life at sea was not for him, he joined the RAF instead. As a Flying Officer, his work was mostly desk-based which caused him little satisfaction. As Guy Phelps, one of the children he rescued when he first arrived in Prague, commented that Chadwick "had a chequered subsequent life and career, at one point joining the RAF where he was both court-martialled and (later) promoted."[175] His disciplinary was due to absence without leave, which was time spent drinking – a hobby which sadly engulfed a lot of his life.

His promotion to Flight Lieutenant was unfortunately short lived, as on 25th February 1942 he crashed his military jeep whilst posted in Africa, and was invalided back to Britain. He was diagnosed with anxiety and depression, resulting in his dismissal for being "found below required standard" for the military.[176]

Life for Chadwick was not particularly happy after this, with his separation from his wife, remarriage and then further separation from his second wife. For 10 years, he worked in various careers, including being a landlord, a driver and working in gambling. After his second divorce, Chadwick became critically ill with tuberculosis, which nearly cost him his life.

It was his move to Norway that put his life back on track. In Oslo, he took on teaching again, before founding the Oslo University Press with friends, which he enjoyed until he retired aged 68 and moved back to Britain.

Back in Southampton Chadwick met Sigi, his third wife, whom he was with for the rest of his life. Sadly Chadwick was again struck down by illness, this time a stroke which led to medical issues in hospital, and his eventual death in 1979, aged 72.

Finally, Doreen Warriner spent the start of the war in London, working for the war effort within the Ministry of Economic Welfare and the Political Warfare Executive. She was the first of the three principle characters to receive any recognition for their work in Prague, being honoured with an OBE in 1941. She was put forward for this award by her close companion and now friend, Robert Stopford, who stated that a large number of refugees "owed their lives to her unremitting devotion to their cause... regardless of the risks she herself ran."[177]

In 1943, Warriner left Britain, and headed for the Middle East, where there was more relief work to be carried out. In her capacity as Chief of the United Nations Relief and Rehabilitation Administration food mission in Yugoslavia for the next two years, she helped save countless further lives.

Returning to Britain in 1946, she re-joined the University College London as a lecturer in the School of Slavonic and East European Studies in 1947. For the next 13 years she lectured in the world's leading research centre on Russia, the Baltics, and Central, Eastern and South-East Europe. In this time, she published many papers, including a dairy of her time in Prague from 1938 to 1939.

In 1965, Warriner was promoted to the role of professor with the UCL, which she continued for seven years. Similar to Chadwick, she died of a stroke aged 68, in 1972.

Like Chadwick and Winton, she did not speak much of the work she carried out in Prague. None boasted that between October 1938 and March 1939, at least 7,000 visas had been issued through the BCRC, which can help us to assume that at least 7,000 people were saved from a predictable death.

As you will have read, so many people were essential to this rescue mission, and it is likely that if just one had not been willing to give up their time, energy and safety to participate, then the whole operation would have failed. It is therefore thanks to the "active goodness" of Winton, Chadwick and Warriner, and so many others, that these men, women and children were saved from death.

ABOUT THE AUTHOR

Born in 1991, Edward Abel Smith grew up in Hertfordshire, before moving to Oxford to study Sociology & Anthropology at Oxford Brookes University. He now lives in London working as a headhunter. This is his first book (and he hopes not his last).

BIBLIOGRAPHY

Chadwick, William, *The Rescue of the Prague Refugees,* Troubador Publishing, *2010*

Cohan, Susan, *Rescue the Perishing. Eleanor Rathbone and the Refugees,* Vallentine Mitchell, 2010

Emanuel, Muriel & Gissing, Vera, *Nicholas Winton and the Rescued Generation*, Vallentine Mitchell, 2002

Gershon, Karen, *We Came As Children. A collective Autobiography of Refugees*, Victor Gollancz Ltd, 1966

Mináč, Matej, *Nicholas Winton's Lottery of Life,* American Friends of the Czech Republic, 2007

Sherman, Ari, *Island Refuge. Britain and Refugees from the Third Reich 1933-1939,* Frank Cass & Co Ltd, 1973

Smith, Lyn, *Heroes of The Holocaust. Ordinary Britons Who Risked Their Lives to Make a Difference,* Ebury Press, 2013

Warriner, Doreen, *Winter in Prague*, SEER, Vol 62, No 2, 1984

Winton, Barbara, *If It's Not Impossible... The Life of Sir Nicholas Winton,* Troubador Publishing Ltd, 2014

ACKNOWLEDGEMENTS

The inspiration and basis for this book has been on three works that must be mentioned. These are the books by Nicolas Winton's daughter, Barbara, Trevor Chadwick's son, William and the diary of Doreen Warriner. All three are exceptional works, and far superior to this book.

QUOTATION SOURCES

[1] Barrow, Becky, *The British Schindler wins knighthood at 93,* The Telegraph, 31.12.2002

[2] Berlin, Lawrence & Fetzer, Anita, *Dialogue in Politics,* John Benjamins Publishing, 2012, p.265

[3] Berlin, Lawrence & Fetzer, Anita, *Dialogue in Politics,* John Benjamins Publishing, 2012, p.265

[4] Carr Begbie, Francis, *The Nicholas Winton Kindertransport Myth Comes Off the Rails,* The Occidental Observer, 2014

[5] Chadwick, William, *The Rescue of the Prague Refugees,* Troubador Publishing, 2010, p.41

[6] Robertson, Connie, *Dictionary of Quotations,* Wordsworth Editions, 1998, p.83

[7] Hitler, Adolf, *Closing speech at the NSDAP congress in Nuremberg,* 1938

[8] Knowles, Elizabeth, *Oxford Dictionary of Quotations,* Oxford University Press, 2004, p.206

[9] Knowles, Elizabeth, *Oxford Dictionary of Quotations,* Oxford University Press, 2004, p.206

[10] Churchill, Winston, *The Gathering Storm,* Rosetta Books LLC, 1948, p.290

[11] Cazalet, Victor, Grenfell, David, Salter, Arthur & Rathbone, Eleanor, *The Birmingham Daily Post,* 04.01.1939

[12] Hitler, Adolf, *Mein Kampf: My Struggle*: (Vol. I & Vol. II) (Complete & Illustrated Edition), eKitap Projesi, 2016 (originally from 1939), Chapter 11

[13] Smith, Lyn, *Heroes of The Holocaust. Ordinary Britons Who Risked Their Lives To Make A Difference,* Ebury Press, 2013, p.52

[14] Koestler, Arthur, *Scum of the Earth,* Eland Publishing Ltd, 2006, p.94

[15] Sherman, Ari, *Island Refuge. Britain and Refugees from the Third Reich 1933-1939,* Frank Cass & Co Ltd, 1973, p.139

[16] Cohan, Susan, *Rescue the Perishing. Eleanor Rathbone and the Refugees, Vallentine* Mitchell, 2010, p.108

[17] Smith, Lyn, *Heroes of The Holocaust. Ordinary Britons Who Risked Their Lives To Make A Difference,* Ebury Press, 2013, p.52

[18] Emanuel, Muriel & Gissing, Vera, *Nicholas Winton and the Rescued Generation*, Vallentine Mitchell, 2002, p.65

[19] Emanuel, Muriel & Gissing, Vera, *Nicholas Winton and the Rescued Generation*, Vallentine Mitchell, 2002, p.65

[20] Chadwick, William, *The Rescue of the Prague Refugees,* Troubador Publishing, *2010,* p.76

[21] Chadwick, William, *The Rescue of the Prague Refugees,* Troubador Publishing, *2010,* p.67

[22] Bourne, Peter, *www.dragonschool.org,* The Dragon School Trust, 2017

[23] Phelps, Guy, *Forgotten Heroes of the Kindertransport,* The Guardian, 03.07.2017

[24] Annual Colonial Reports, *Nigeria Report for 1930,* His Majesty's Stationary Office, 1931, p.7

[25] Chadwick, William, *The Rescue of the Prague Refugees,* Troubador Publishing, 2010, p.68

[26] Chadwick, William, *The Rescue of the Prague Refugees,* Troubador Publishing, 2010, p.70

[27] Yorkshire Post, *Queen Pays Tribute to 'British Schindler'* 11.03.2003

[28] Winton, Barbara, *If It's Not Impossible... The Life of Sir Nicholas Winton,* Troubador Publishing Ltd, 2014, p.49

[29] Stowe School, *The Official Opening of Stanhope House,* Stowe School Ltd 2009 – 2011

[30] Winton, Barbara, *If It's Not Impossible... The Life of Sir Nicholas Winton*, Troubador Publishing Ltd, 2014, p.72

[31] Winton, Barbara, *If It's Not Impossible... The Life of Sir Nicholas Winton*, Troubador Publishing Ltd, 2014, p.72

[32] Levine, Gary, *Inner Greatness: How Nicholas Winton and Doreen Warriner Saved the World,* Naples Herald, 2015

[33] Malvern St James Girls School, www.malvernstjames.co.uk, 2017

[34] Gwyer, Barbara, *Association of Senior Members, Chronicles 1928 – 29,* St Hugh's College, Oxford, 2015

[35] Warriner, Doreen, *Winter in Prague*, SEER, Vol 62, No 2, 1984, p.209

[36] Hastings, Max, *The Secret War. Spies, Codes and Guerrillas 1939-45,* HarperCollins, 2015, p.2

[37] Warriner, Doreen, *Winter in Prague*, SEER, Vol 62, No 2, 1984, p.211

[38] Hastings, Max, *The Secret War. Spies, Codes and Guerrillas 1939-45,* HarperCollins, 2015, p.40

[39] Warriner, Doreen, *Winter in Prague*, SEER, Vol 62, No 2, 1984, p.211

[40] Chadwick, William, *The Rescue of Prague Refugees,* Troubador Publishing, 2010, p.5

[41] Sherman, Ari, *Island Refuge. Britain and Refugees from the Third Reich 1933-1939,* Frank Cass & Co Ltd, 1973, p.139

[42] Refugee's Thanksgiving Painting of M.P, *Birmingham Daily Gazette,* 17.06.1939

[43] Warriner, Doreen, *Winter in Prague*, SEER, Vol 62, No 2, 1984, p.212

[44] Warriner, Doreen, *Winter in Prague*, SEER, Vol 62, No 2, 1984, p.213

45 Waldron, Arthur, *How Peace Was Lost: The 1935 Memorandum: Developments Affecting American Policy in the Far East,* Hoover Press, 2000, p.75

[46] Warriner, Doreen, *Winter in Prague*, SEER, Vol 62, No 2, 1984, p.213

[47] The Telegraph, Obituary – Jean Rowntree, 05.03.2003

[48] Warriner, Doreen, *Winter in Prague*, SEER, Vol 62, No 2, 1984, p.213

[49] Gershon, Karen, *We Came as Children. A collective Autobiography of Refugees,* Victor Gollancz Ltd, 1966, p.150

[50] Cazalet, Victor, Grenfell, David, Salter, Arthur & Rathbone, Eleanor, *The Birmingham Daily Post,* 04.01.1939

[51] Brown, Martin D, *A Munich Winter or a Prague Spring? The evolution of British policy towards the Sudeten Germans from October 1938 to September 1939,* http://www.academia.edu

[52] Western Daily Press, 02.11.1938

[53] Lerski, Jerzy Jan, *Historical Dictionary of Poland, 966-1945,* Greenwood Publishing Group, 1996, p.680

[54] Warriner, Doreen, *Winter in Prague*, SEER, Vol 62, No 2, 1984, p.217

[55] Melvern, Linda, *Obituary: Lord Hankey,* The Independent, 1996

[56] Chadwick, William, *The Rescue of the Prague Refugees,* Troubador Publishing, 2010, p.11

[57] Warriner, Doreen, *Winter in Prague*, SEER, Vol 62, No 2, 1984, p.216

[58] Chadwick, William, *The Rescue of the Prague Refugees,* Troubador Publishing, *2010,* p.9

[59] Chadwick, William, *The Rescue of the Prague Refugees,* Troubador Publishing, *2010,* p.12

[60] Warriner, Doreen, *Winter in Prague*, SEER, Vol 62, No 2, 1984, p.217

[61] Emanuel, Muriel & Gissing, Vera, *Nicholas Winton and the Rescued Generation*, Vallentine Mitchell, 2002, p.65

[62] Warriner, Doreen, *Winter in Prague*, SEER, Vol 62, No 2, 1984, p.218

[63] Mináč, Matej, *Nicholas Winton's Lottery of Life*, American Friends of the Czech Republic, 2007, p.77

[64] Mináč, Matej, *Nicholas Winton's Lottery of Life*, American Friends of the Czech Republic, 2007, p.75

[65] Winton, Barbara, *If It's Not Impossible... The Life of Sir Nicholas Winton*, Troubador Publishing Ltd, 2014, p.17

[66] Emanuel, Muriel & Gissing, Vera, *Nicholas Winton and the Rescued Generation*, Vallentine Mitchell, 2002, p.71

[67] Winton, Barbara, *If It's Not Impossible... The Life of Sir Nicholas Winton*, Troubador Publishing Ltd, 2014, p.20

[68] Winton, Barbara, *If It's Not Impossible... The Life of Sir Nicholas Winton*, Troubador Publishing Ltd, 2014, p.18

[69] Chadwick, William, *The Rescue of the Prague Refugees*, Troubador Publishing, 2010, p.40

[70] Winton, Barbara, *If It's Not Impossible... The Life of Sir Nicholas Winton*, Troubador Publishing Ltd, 2014, p.19

[71] Winton, Barbara, *If It's Not Impossible... The Life of Sir Nicholas Winton*, Troubador Publishing Ltd, 2014, p.19

[72] Chadwick, William, *The Rescue of the Prague Refugees*, Troubador Publishing, 2010, p.40

[73] Winton, Barbara, *If It's Not Impossible... The Life of Sir Nicholas Winton*, Troubador Publishing Ltd, 2014, p.20

[74] Mináč, Matej, *Nicholas Winton's Lottery of Life*, American Friends of the Czech Republic, 2007, p.141

[75] Chadwick, William, *The Rescue of the Prague Refugees*, Troubador Publishing, 2010, p.8

[76] Winton, Barbara, *If It's Not Impossible... The Life of Sir Nicholas Winton,* Troubador Publishing Ltd, 2014, p.23

[77] Winton, Barbara, *If It's Not Impossible... The Life of Sir Nicholas Winton,* Troubador Publishing Ltd, 2014, p.23

[78] Cohan, Susan, *Rescue the Perishing. Eleanor Rathbone and the Refugees, Vallentine* Mitchell, 2010, p.116

[79] Warriner, Doreen, *Winter in Prague*, SEER, Vol 62, No 2, 1984, p.222

[80] Warriner, Doreen, *Winter in Prague*, SEER, Vol 62, No 2, 1984, p.219

[81] Warriner, Doreen, *Winter in Prague*, SEER, Vol 62, No 2, 1984, p.220

[82] Gershon, Karen, *We Came as Children. A collective Autobiography of Refugees,* Victor Gollancz Ltd, 1966, p.22

[83] Gershon, Karen, *We came as Children. A collective Autobiography of Refugees,* Victor Gollancz Ltd, 1966, p.22

[84] Warriner, Doreen, *Winter in Prague*, SEER, Vol 62, No 2, 1984, p.223

[85] Winton, Barbara, *If It's Not Impossible... The Life of Sir Nicholas Winton,* Troubador Publishing Ltd, 2014, p.25

[86] Emanuel, Muriel & Gissing, Vera, *Nicholas Winton and the Rescued Generation*, Vallentine Mitchell, 2002, p.73

[87] Winton, Barbara, *If It's Not Impossible... The Life of Sir Nicholas Winton,* Troubador Publishing Ltd, 2014, p.27

[88] Winton, Barbara, *If It's Not Impossible... The Life of Sir Nicholas Winton,* Troubador Publishing Ltd, 2014, p.27

[89] Winton, Barbara, *If It's Not Impossible... The Life of Sir Nicholas Winton,* Troubador Publishing Ltd, 2014, p.33

[90] Winton, Barbara, *If It's Not Impossible... The Life of Sir Nicholas Winton,* Troubador Publishing Ltd, 2014, p.35

[91] Winton, Barbara, *If It's Not Impossible... The Life of Sir Nicholas Winton,* Troubador Publishing Ltd, 2014, p.35

EDWARD ABEL SMITH

[92] Mináč, Matej, *Nicholas Winton's Lottery of Life,* American Friends of the Czech Republic, 2007, p.106.

[93] Warriner, Doreen, *Winter in Prague*, SEER, Vol 62, No 2, 1984, p.222

[94] Warriner, Doreen, *Winter in Prague*, SEER, Vol 62, No 2, 1984, p.222

[95] Chadwick, William, *The Rescue of the Prague Refugees,* Troubador Publishing, *2010,* p.23

[96] Warriner, Doreen, *Winter in Prague*, SEER, Vol 62, No 2, 1984, p.224

[97] Mináč, Matej, *Nicholas Winton's Lottery of Life,* American Friends of the Czech Republic, 2007, p.38

[98] Warriner, Doreen, *Winter in Prague*, SEER, Vol 62, No 2, 1984, p.225

[99] Warriner, Doreen, *Winter in Prague*, SEER, Vol 62, No 2, 1984, p.225

[100] Warriner, Doreen, *Winter in Prague*, SEER, Vol 62, No 2, 1984, p.225

[101] Jaksch, Wenzel, *Farewell to Bohemia,* www.radio.cz, 2011

[102] Warriner, Doreen, *Winter in Prague*, SEER, Vol 62, No 2, 1984, p.226

[103] Warriner, Doreen, *Winter in Prague*, SEER, Vol 62, No 2, 1984, p.226

[104] Warriner, Doreen, *Winter in Prague*, SEER, Vol 62, No 2, 1984, p.226

[105] Cadbury, Tessa, *Oral History,* from www.iwm.org.uk/collections/item/object/80013904, 1994

[106] Gershon, Karen, *We Came as Children. A collective Autobiography of Refugees,* Victor Gollancz Ltd, 1966, p.24

[107] Warriner, Doreen, *Winter in Prague*, SEER, Vol 62, No 2, 1984, p.234

[108] Winton, Barbara, *If It's Not Impossible... The Life of Sir Nicholas Winton,* Troubador Publishing Ltd, 2014, p.29

[109] Winton, Barbara, *If It's Not Impossible... The Life of Sir Nicholas Winton,* Troubador Publishing Ltd, 2014, p.29

[110] Warriner, Doreen, *Winter in Prague*, SEER, Vol 62, No 2, 1984, p.231

[111] Daily Herald, 09.05.1939

[112] Warriner, Doreen, *Winter in Prague*, SEER, Vol 62, No 2, 1984, p.231

[113] Warriner, Doreen, *Winter in Prague*, SEER, Vol 62, No 2, 1984, p.231

[114] Jaksch, Wenzel, *Farewell to Bohemia,* www.radio.cz, 2011

[115] Brown, Martin D, *A Munich Winter or a Prague Spring? The evolution of British policy towards the Sudeten Germans from October 1938 to September 1939,* http://www.academia.edu

[116] Warriner, Doreen, *Winter in Prague*, SEER, Vol 62, No 2, 1984, p.231

[117] Warriner, Doreen, *Winter in Prague*, SEER, Vol 62, No 2, 1984, p.231

[118] Chadwick, William, *The Rescue of the Prague Refugees,* Troubador Publishing, *2010,* p.30

[119] Jaksch, Wenzel, *Farewell to Bohemia,* www.radio.cz, 2011

[120] Jaksch, Wenzel, *Farewell to Bohemia,* www.radio.cz, 2011

[121] Jaksch, Wenzel, *Farewell to Bohemia,* www.radio.cz, 2011

[122] Daily Herald, 09.05.1939

[123] Jaksch, Wenzel, *Farewell to Bohemia,* www.radio.cz, 2011

[124] Bachstein, Martin, *Wenzel Jaksch und die Sudentendeutsche Sozialdemokratie,* R. Oldenbourg, 1974, p.183

[125] Jaksch, Wenzel, *Farewell to Bohemia,* www.radio.cz, 2011

[126] Jaksch, Wenzel, *Farewell to Bohemia,* www.radio.cz, 2011

[127] Jaksch, Wenzel, *Farewell to Bohemia,* www.radio.cz, 2011

[128] Jaksch, Wenzel, *Farewell to Bohemia,* www.radio.cz, 2011

[129] Warriner, Doreen, *Winter in Prague*, SEER, Vol 62, No 2, 1984, p.231

[130] Jaksch, Wenzel, *Farewell to Bohemia,* www.radio.cz, 2011

[131] Jaksch, Wenzel, *Farewell to Bohemia,* www.radio.cz, 2011

[132] Warriner, Doreen, *Winter in Prague*, SEER, Vol 62, No 2, 1984, p.231

[133] Warriner, Doreen, *Winter in Prague*, SEER, Vol 62, No 2, 1984, p.231

[134] Warriner, Doreen, *Winter in Prague*, SEER, Vol 62, No 2, 1984, p.231

[135] Bachstein, Martin, *Wenzel Jaksch und die Sudentendeutsche Sozialdemokratie,* R. Oldenbourg, 1974, p.183

[136] Hardwick, Steve & Hodgin, Duane E., *WWII Duty, Honor, Country. The Memories of Those Who Were There,* iUniverse, 2012, p.5

[137] Warriner, Doreen, *Winter in Prague*, SEER, Vol 62, No 2, 1984, p.233

[138] Warriner, Doreen, *Winter in Prague*, SEER, Vol 62, No 2, 1984, p.233

[139] Warriner, Doreen, *Winter in Prague*, SEER, Vol 62, No 2, 1984, p.233

[140] Warriner, Doreen, *Winter in Prague*, SEER, Vol 62, No 2, 1984, p.233

[141] Warriner, Doreen, *Winter in Prague*, SEER, Vol 62, No 2, 1984, p.236

[142] McDonough, Frank, *The Gestapo. The Myth and Reality of Hitler's Secret Police,"* Coronet, 2015, p.56

[143] McDonough, Frank, *The Gestapo. The Myth and Reality of Hitler's Secret Police,"* Coronet, 2015, p.56

[144] Chadwick, William, *The Rescue of the Prague Refugees,* Troubador Publishing, 2010, p.122

[145] Milton, Giles, *The Ministry of Ungentlemanly Warfare. Churchill's Mavericks: Plotting Hitler's Defeat,* John Murray Publishers, 2016, *p.*190

[146] Warriner, Doreen, *Winter in Prague*, SEER, Vol 62, No 2, 1984, p.237

[147] Warriner, Doreen, *Winter in Prague*, SEER, Vol 62, No 2, 1984, p.236

[148] Warriner, Doreen, *Winter in Prague*, SEER, Vol 62, No 2, 1984, p.236

[149] Gershon, Karen, *We Came as Children. A collective Autobiography of Refugees, Victor Gollancz Ltd*, 1966, p.25

[150] Newcastle Evening Chronicle, 14.08.1939

[151] Gershon, Karen, *We Came as Children. A collective Autobiography of Refugees, Victor Gollancz Ltd*, 1966, p.24

[152] Winton, Barbara, *If It's Not Impossible... The Life of Sir Nicholas Winton,* Troubador Publishing Ltd, 2014, p.30

[153] Gershon, Karen, *We Came as Children. A collective Autobiography of Refugees*, Victor Gollancz Ltd, 1966, p.24

[154] Gershon, Karen, *We Came as Children. A collective Autobiography of Refugees*, Victor Gollancz Ltd, 1966, p.24

[155] Chadwick, William, *The Rescue of the Prague Refugees,* Troubador Publishing, *2010,* p.79

[156] Chadwick, William, *The Rescue of the Prague Refugees,* Troubador Publishing, *2010,* p.83

[157] Mináč, Matej, *Nicholas Winton's Lottery of Life,* American Friends of the Czech Republic, 2007, p.219.

[158] Brown, Martin D, *A Munich Winter or a Prague Spring? The evolution of British policy towards the Sudeten Germans from October 1938 to September 1939,* http://www.academia.edu

[159] Duffy, Carole Ann, *Older and Wiser: Carole Ann Duffy introduces poems of aging*, The Guardian, 13.03.2010

[160] Hahn, Fred, *Slavic Review,* 27.01.2017

[161] Hartlepool Northern Daily Mail, 02.08.1957

[162] Warriner, Doreen, *Winter in Prague*, SEER, Vol 62, No 2, 1984, p.211

[163] Tombs, Isabelle, *The Victory of Socialist 'Vansittartism': Labour and the German Question, 1941–5,* from 20 Century British History volume 7 (issue 3) 1996 p.287

[164] Pelling, Henry, *Churchill's Peacetime Ministry, 1951-55,* Macmillan Press Ltd, 1997, p.12

[165] Gloucestershire Echo, 05.06.1943

[166] Melvern, Linda, *Obituary: Lord Hankey,* The Independent, 1996

[167] Sunderland Daily Echo and Shipping Gazette, 11.12.1942

[168] Warriner, Doreen, *Winter in Prague*, SEER, Vol 62, No 2, 1984, p.213

[169] Yorkshire Evening Post, *Miss Rowntree Engaged,* 06.07.1942

[170] Warriner, Doreen, *Winter in Prague*, SEER, Vol 62, No 2, 1984, p.217

[171] Barrow, Becky, *The British Schindler wins knighthood at 93,* The Telegraph, 31.12.2002

[172] Winton, Barbara, *If It's Not Impossible... The Life of Sir Nicholas Winton,* Troubador Publishing Ltd, 2014, p.123

[173] Winton, Barbara, *If It's Not Impossible... The Life of Sir Nicholas Winton,* Troubador Publishing Ltd, 2014, p.173

[174] Winton, Nicholas, *What Makes a Hero? A letter from Nicholas Winton,* Holocaust Education Trust 28.03.1999

[175] Phelps, Guy, *Forgotten Heroes of the Kindertransport,* The Guardian, 03.07.2017

[176] Chadwick, William, *The Rescue of the Prague Refugees,* Troubador Publishing, *2010,* p.85

[177] Chadwick, William, *The Rescue of the Prague Refugees,* Troubador Publishing, *2010,* p.36

Printed in Great Britain
by Amazon

36591831R00111